CLASSROOM LEARNING CENTERS

Classroom Learning Centers

Planning, Organization, Materials, and Activities

JOHN E. MORLAN

CONTRIBUTING AUTHORS

LEONARD J. ESPINOSA
ALLEN C. FRIEBEL
WELDON W. PARKER
ROBERT J. RAMONDA

David S. Lake Publishers
BELMONT, CALIFORNIA

Copyright ©1974 by David S. Lake Publishers, 19 Davis Drive, Belmont, California 94002. All rights reserved. No part of this book may be reproduced by any means, transmitted, or translated into a machine language without written permission from the publisher.

Library of Congress Catalog Card Number: 73-777592

ISBN 0-8224-1410-4

Printed in the United States of America.

Editor: Lesley Anne Swanson

Designer: Eleanor Mennick

Illustrators: Rudy Iseger, Cyndy Hamilton

Preface

For years teachers have been concerned about how they may better provide for student initiative and involvement in the learning process. Now a nationwide emphasis on providing for individual differences has motivated many teachers to seek ways of personalizing education. It is the aim of this book to provide a way to help meet the learning needs of children through an exciting, practical approach to education.

Several professors at California State University, San Jose, have been working with teachers as they have developed the classroom learning center approach to education, and have contributed materials included in this book. Dr. Espinosa made major contributions to Chapter 2. Dr. Friebel wrote Chapters 5, 8, and 9. Dr. Parker wrote Chapter 6, and Dr. Ramonda wrote Chapters 4 and 7. My contributions were Chapters 1, 2, 3, and overseeing editing of the manuscript throughout.

It is our hope that both pre-service and in-service teachers will find this book to be a useful guide as they attempt to personalize instruction through classroom learning centers.

San Jose, California

JOHN E. MORLAN

Contents

SECTION I

Planning and Organization

MORE AND MORE teachers are turning to classroom learning centers as a means of making learning more vital, alive, and personal for their students. Classroom learning centers call for the continuous, personal involvement of students, and if properly implemented they allow for individual differences in learning rates and developmental levels as well.

Classroom learning centers include materials, equipment, and learning space so arranged that children in one class can work at a variety of learning tasks simultaneously. For example, at any given moment, children in one room might be studying contemporary Africa through map exercises; learning new vocabulary words by playing reading games with friends; manipulating cubes to gain an understanding of volume; performing an experiment with mealworms and cereal; or writing dialogue for a historical drama. The child may be a member of a small group or committee of students who are viewing a film, or he may work alone, listening to a tape recording as he follows a guide sheet in an audio-tutorial approach to learning. While most of the children work independently at classroom learning centers, the teacher is free to tutor an individual child or a small group of children who need her help in solving learning problems.

Learning centers can serve a variety of purposes. They can help students gain factual knowledge, develop specific skills, deepen understanding, and spark creative activities in as many areas as imagination and interest permit.

Kinds of Classroom Learning Centers

Classroom learning centers are usually designated by the subject matter they emphasize, the kind of media they involve, or the type of activity they present. Learning centers can also be organized from the standpoint of several levels of a single activity, such as the development of specific skills, attitudes and appreciations, and creative expression. In addition, special centers may be established temporarily to capitalize on current interests or events.

Subject matter. When establishing classroom learning centers, teachers usually select some themes from traditional subject matter areas. The teaching of math, science, language arts, reading, spelling, social studies, art, and music can all be enhanced by learning centers. Even physical education can be taught in this manner.

Media. Learning centers can be designated according to the media they incorporate. The audio center for listening or audio-tutorial activities, for example, can be used to introduce topics as diverse as word attack skills, fractions, or friction. A projection-viewing center can be equally flexible. When not in use, media centers can double as activity areas to be used by small groups or individuals working on special projects.

Activity. Students can try all forms of creative writing at an author's center. A drill center can be set up for those needing repeated practice in selected skills. Construction, painting, and sculpting activities belong in an artist's center. A discovery center can be established to foster inquiry and the use of the scientific method. Children can also benefit from a well-planned and well-stocked game center that provides for the development and application of reading and mathematics skills.

When first deciding what kinds of centers to use, it is best to select a combination of all three types—subject, media, and activity—that suit the needs of both the teacher and the children. Later, if a particular center is not used as much as was expected, it can be modified to double for two or more activities. Remember that children may occasionally need to work alone or with only one other child. It is wise to provide for this need, too, in arranging the classroom. Specific examples of activities, materials, and the learning center approach to the teaching of selected subjects can be found in Section II. They will provide practical assistance to the teacher who plans to establish learning centers in her classroom.

The Teacher's Role

Once the classroom learning centers are in operation, the teacher's role shifts from serving as a chief information officer to becoming a kind of classroom manager—a much more professional and demanding task. The teaching skills used in a traditional setting are still needed here, but their emphasis and application have changed. The teacher must now be able to do the following:

Determine where in the instructional scheme learning centers may be used in combination with more traditional large-group and small-group instruction.

Establish behavioral objectives to help determine what kinds of centers will be most beneficial, considering her own approach to teaching and the needs of the children.

Determine alternate room arrangements. This aspect of establishing learning centers will be explained at length later in this chapter.

Plan a sequence of activities based upon student need, taking into account the learning style, learning rate, and other individual characteristics of children.

Plan for variety among the centers in order to maintain a high level of interest and motivation. This means determining what materials and equipment can be obtained from existing supplies, as well as constructing a wide range of new teaching materials.

Develop an evaluation and record-keeping system that will help determine the children's academic achievement and progress, as well as provide the diagnostic information needed to correct deficiencies and promote growth.

Select and make learning materials, or supervise their construction.

Write teaching contracts that will aid in guiding the children's learning activities.

Develop storage and check-out systems for materials that are used in the centers.

Develop inventory check procedures which show at a glance that all materials are present, that some materials are missing and need to be replaced, or that other materials are damaged and need to be repaired.

Design an assignment board that shows each child's daily schedule. Allow each child to work at a number of centers during the day and during the week so that he will have an overall balance of learning experiences.

Develop basic skills in positive reinforcement techniques along with other counseling procedures.

The Student's Role

In addition to the responsibilities he has for learning in the traditional setting, the child who works at learning centers will:

Develop skills of self-management so that he learns how to learn as the program unfolds.

Develop independence through activities that involve exploration and discovery.

Learn to work with other students in both small and large group settings, and develop sensitivity to their needs.

Learn how to sequence his learning activities during the day and during the week.

Learn to live up to a commitment made to the teacher and to himself by carrying out the terms of teaching-learning contracts used in conjunction with learning center activities.

Develop specialized skills, talents, and interests by selecting many of his own assignments.

Pay more attention to his schoolwork because it is at a level appropriate for him, neither as frustrating nor as boring as the traditional approach.

Develop skills of self-evaluation and record his own progress. Subject area or activity folders can be kept in each center, and all students can place their papers in the folder, completed and checked as appropriate. Or each student may have a personal folder that holds all his work from all centers and activities. Combinations of these methods can also be developed.

Lesson Development

If learning center lessons are to succeed, teachers need to be more certain of what they want to teach and much more precise in assessing individual achievement than is usually the case in traditional classrooms. Keep the following suggestions in mind while developing lessons:

1. *List the behavioral objectives you hold for the student.* What should he know? What should he understand? What skills should he master? What evidence will you have that he has learned what you want him to learn? The answers to these questions will help you focus on specific skills, concepts, and creative activities. As you list each objective, you may wish to write evaluation questions or activities designed to measure student progress in that area. If you list each behavioral objective and each evaluation question separately on 5" × 7" cards, you can shuffle the sets until a satisfactory sequence is established.[1]

2. *List all activities and materials needed to complete each objective.* In some instances, written directions or illustrations may be sufficient to guide learning. In other instances, films, filmstrips, and audio materials may be necessary. Realia such as plants and seeds often prove to be valuable tools. At other times manipulative materials, reference books, basic readers, or worksheets may be needed. Try to vary your approach to learning, and use multi-media activities whenever possible.

3. *Plan a method for checking student progress.* Both you and the student need specific feedback on a regular basis. Be sure to include a lesson record and evaluation system that both of you understand.

[1]Jerrold Kemp's book, *Instructional Design* (Belmont, Calif.: Fearon Publishers/Lear Siegler, Inc., 1971), is an inexpensive, easy-to-read, and practical guide to lesson development.

4. *Try out new materials on an average student* from your class before integrating them into the learning program. That way, you will be able to make appropriate adjustments in vocabulary and content, and you can estimate how long it will take your students to complete that activity. In addition, it is often helpful to have another teacher look over what you have planned.

5. *Develop the attitude that if the children have difficulty with a lesson, the fault probably lies in the material.* Note where difficulties arise, help the children as necessary, then revise the lesson when time permits. Difficulties are to to be expected when new materials are introduced, so don't be discouraged when they arise.

Evaluation and Record Keeping

In order to be successful, classroom learning centers must be planned to meet specific needs. For this reason, determination of student development levels through diagnostic techniques is essential. If multi-level materials are provided, the student may select from among the alternatives those materials best suited to his needs.

EVALUATION

The following list describes the means of diagnosis most likely to meet specific classroom needs. In addition to these items, the material in each child's cumulative folder may contain helpful information.

1. *Health records* list any physical disabilities which may limit a child's participation in certain activities. Close work with school health personnel—school nurse, psychologist, vision and audio screening specialists—will help you spot physical limitations that might otherwise go unnoticed.

2. *Teacher-made diagnostic tests* help to determine skill levels (particularly in reading and math). Tests to go with specific units of work, and to check general achievement are most useful. If the student shows he has already mastered a skill, he may skip that unit of work and advance to something more challenging. Or, if the unit seems too difficult, the student may work at a lower level, with more teacher and peer assistance, until he develops proficiency.

3. *Standardized tests* are useful in determining general placement levels as a starting point for study. Specific unit tests, teacher observation, and informal inventories, however, should be used in conjunction with standardized test results. These serve only as guidelines for getting started.

4. *Interest inventories* that indicate student interest, likes, and dislikes are useful in assigning activities and may help the teacher motivate a reluctant learner.

5. *Previous teachers' appraisals* of the children may suggest useful ways of working with individuals, particularly those who have adjustment problems. These

appraisals are often quite subjective and should be treated with caution; personality conflicts between teacher and student may cause a biased assessment. In spite of their limitations, however, these evaluations may help shed some light on a child's personality problems.

6. *Classroom discussions and individual interviews* may bring out unsuspected aspects of each child's self-image and indicate which children feel insecure. Psychological tests can be quite helpful in understanding children who exhibit abnormal behavior.

RECORD KEEPING

The following systems have proven to be useful in recording student progress:

Subject folder. Each child places his finished papers or creative work in a class folder at the center. It is then ready to be checked by you at the end of the period or at the end of the day.

Individual student folder. Store this folder in a box, file drawer, record rack, or other central location, but never in the student's desk where materials may easily be damaged or lost. Each child is responsible for filing his own papers after they have been corrected. Check through folder materials periodically to make sure they are being corrected properly.

Report file book. Provide a ring binder at each class-room learning center for students to file summaries of their activities, reports, observations, experiments, and other kinds of written work. Tape a class record chart to the inside front cover of the binder or folder. List the students' names down the left side of the page, and the tasks or activities across the top of the page (Fig. 1-1). As each student completes each item, he places a check mark with pencil in the space provided. If you think the work is satisfactory, check the same square with ink. If the work is below standard, erase the child's check mark. An erasure indicates that the child should consult with you about additional learning experiences in that area. Keep a report file book at each learning center so the children can file their work as soon as it is completed.

Student record book. A student record book contains one sheet of paper for each student in each area. These sheets, marked with columns and check points for all center activities, are useful for keeping track of where students are now and what they need to do next. The student record book is generally kept near the learning center so it is easily accessible to the students.

Contract folder. The student record sheets used with the contract teaching method make an excellent record-keeping system when used in combination with other methods. Contracts may be filed according to subject or activity, or a combination of the two. You may want to keep a bonus folder for students who do extra work.

Wall charts. Charts of various kinds can be used at classroom learning centers for assigning children to specific activities and for displaying learning materials.

The task record chart is structured much like the sheet used in connection with the report file book. Using a black nylon or felt-tip pen, children check off tasks as they complete them. Periodically you should check the chart and files, marking the same square in colored ink if the work is satisfactory and the child is ready to proceed to another task. Erasure of the child's check mark indicates that the child should see you for additional help or remediation. Marks can be erased easily because the chart is covered with plastic.

To make a resuable wall chart, draw horizontal lines about one inch apart on a 28" × 46" piece of railroad board, starting 4 inches from the top. Draw several vertical lines making one column for each task. Cover the chart with clear plastic and tape it on all sides or laminate it with a layer of transparent adhesive shelf paper or laminating plastic. Students can mark on the plastic with water-soluble inks and erase the marks easily with a damp cloth. Marks from a grease pencil can be wiped off with a dry cloth or tissue. It is best to list the tasks and names on the plastic so the chart can be reused.

Developmental task sheet. Jean Piaget, Swiss psychologist, emphasizes the importance of recognizing children's developmental stages. Each child passes through these stages at his own rate. Be sure to observe the children carefully as they work on various developmental tasks and provide them with the materials and the environment that will help them proceed to higher levels of development when they are ready. A developmental

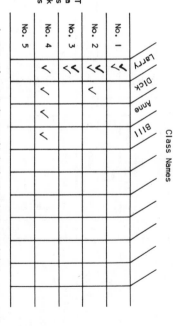

	Larry	Dick	Anne	Bill	Class Names			
No. 1	✓							
No. 2	✓	✓						
No. 3	✓	✓						
No. 4	✓	✓	✓	✓				
No. 5			✓	✓				

Tasks

√ student's mark in pencil indicates task completed

✔ teacher's mark in pen indicates task checked
Teacher's erasure of pencilled check mark means that the student should see the teacher.

FIG. 1-1 *Task record chart*

task checksheet not only helps you keep track of each child's progress, but is of interest to parents as well at conference time. The example in Fig. 1-2, designed for kindergarten and first grade, can be modified to meet the needs of other teaching-learning situations.

File boxes. Student work folders can be stored at each center in a cardboard file box cut to size. Using this system, each child can have his own folder at each center. Children are responsible for filing their own work after they have checked it against an answer key, or after you have checked it yourself. One file box might be labeled *checked,* and a second file box *not checked.*

Classroom learning center materials, arranged or programmed in a logical sequence that allows students to check and correct their own work, are invaluable aids for the busy teacher. Modifications of the systems suggested here may be worked out to suit individual teaching styles.

Organizing Instructional Space

Whether she works in a conventional classroom building or in one of the newer buildings designed for flexibility in arrangement and use of space, the teacher must organize her instructional materials and arrange the furniture to provide for a variety of activity areas. Room arrangement is basic to the success of the learning center program. Before beginning to move the furniture, it is

Name ___	Birthdate ___	Handedness ___
MATCHING	LISTENING	CONCEPTUAL
colors	understands what he hears	assigns no. value
forms	sits still	identifies position in space
sizes	responds to signals	serial order
symbols	follows directions	orders numbers
designs	understands story sequence	recognizes likeness & difference
words	SPEAKING	classifies objects
MEMORY	lacks speech defects	VISUAL MOTOR
writes name	uses complete sentences	tracing
writes numerals	expresses himself clearly	copying
writes letters	learns & uses new words	cutting
COORDINATION	dictates stories	tying
balancing	has acceptable usage	left-to-right sequence
skipping	assigns names to symbols	PHONICS
jumping rope	colors	rhyming sounds
ball skills	shapes	beginning sounds
left and right	numerals	
	own name	
	color words	

Fig. 1-2 *Development task checksheet*

often helpful to look around the rooms of other teachers who use learning centers. If you are to be the pioneer in your school, however, it is best to begin with an inventory.

THE INVENTORY

Because the physical layout of your classroom or learning space will determine in large part the arrangement of your furniture, it is important to note the location of all permanent fixtures. Some of the things you should look for are listed below. It may be helpful to draw a floor plan of your room, roughly to scale, on a ditto master and then sketch in the permanent fixtures. If you run off a dozen copies on the ditto, you can try a dozen different furniture arrangements without moving even one chair. On the ditto master, note the location of the following items:

Doors and windows. It is important to arrange the furniture so that the flow of traffic in and out of the classroom is not obstructed by chairs, tables, cabinets, portable bulletin boards, or other obstacles. Centers set aside for the use of filmstrips or motion picture projectors should be located where no direct light will fall on the screen.

Electrical outlets. These small items are of major importance in room arrangements that provide for the use of audio equipment, projectors, and other electrically powered devices. Cords should not be strung across doorways, over shelves, around rugs, or anywhere children might trip on them. The safety of materials, equipment, and children is an all-important consideration.

Closet space. When the weather is inclement, it is essential that children have direct access from the outside door to the closet space, so they do not have to thread their way through a maze of furniture while wearing coats and boots. Be sure that all closet doors can open completely without disturbing children working at nearby learning centers. If there are doors on the supply closet, remember that both you and the children will need easy access to materials throughout the day. In some cases, it may be best to remove closet doors entirely if they are in the way.

Sinks and counters. Many creative activities will require immediate soap and water cleanup of children and equipment. Science experiences often call for water or the mixing or measuring of liquids. As you design alternate room arrangements, be sure to allow for a traffic pattern that gives children easy access to the sink from both the science and art areas.

Shelf space. The location and extent of built-in shelf space will help you determine where to set up many of your learning centers. Resource materials should be located near the centers where they will be used.

Counters. Three-dimensional art work, math projects, and library books can all be displayed on built-in counters. Instructional materials and games can be stored here as well, and motivating materials used to interest children in a particular unit or module of instruction can be arranged in eye-catching array.

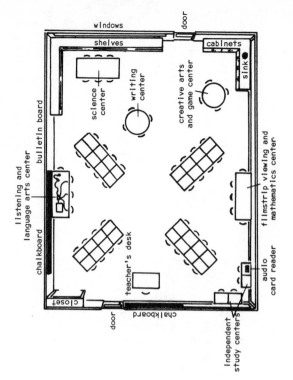

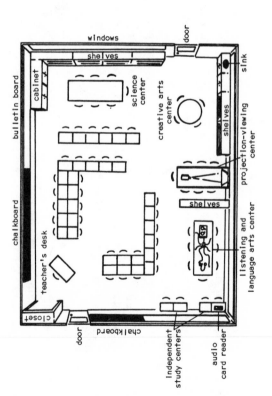

Fɪɢ. 1-3 *Classroom arrangements*

Carpet and tile areas. Many of the newer classrooms have carpeted floors with one area, covered in tile, set aside for art and science activities. The carpeted areas, which help to muffle sound, are ideal for seminars and large group discussions. The tiled areas, easier to clean, are best for projects involving water, wood shavings, sand, paint, nails, or other materials that scatter easily and get lost in the carpet. If the classroom is completely carpeted, inexpensive plywood panels may be used in place of tile for these activities.

Sample Classroom Arrangements

When you have drawn all the permanent fixtures in your classroom or learning space on the ditto master, run off a few copies. Then, with a stack of empty classrooms at your fingertips, study the sample classroom arrangements in Figs. 1-3 through 1-5. These samples include the more common grouping patterns and newer ones as well. After deciding what kinds of equipment and materials you want to use (see Chapter 3) and the specific applications of learning centers and activities to various subject areas (see Section II), you will be ready to draw up several alternate plans that meet your needs. You may decide to modify your classroom layout little by little until a pattern particularly suited to your teaching style is achieved. Whatever plan you choose, move slowly enough to maintain control of your classroom activities during the transition period.

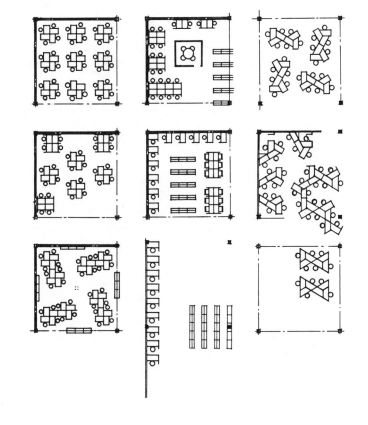

Fig. 1-4 *Additional seating arrangements (courtesy Educational Facilities Laboratories and The School Library)*

Organizing Materials and Supplies

Successful individualized instruction using classroom learning centers and contract teaching depends on many factors. One of the most important of these is the organization of materials and supplies. Consider the following items carefully before arranging your learning centers:

1. Books and other resource materials in a variety of media are easy to locate if they are grouped by subject. All materials for math, for example, whether realia, blocks, filmstrips, models, or books, should be located in the same general area of the room. Use large, easy-to-read labels to designate these areas. In the lower primary grades, use drawings or pictures instead.

2. Assemble kits containing all the materials necessary to complete assigned tasks. Store them in cardboard boxes labeled accordingly. If one center must be used for a number of activities, each set of materials can be stored in a box, then moved quickly to the center when it is needed. When the task has been completed, the children can simply put the materials back in the box, and they will be ready for storage once more. Each box should contain directions for using the materials it contains, whether supplies, books, or worksheets. If possible, provide a variety of activities from which the children may choose in order to reach the same instructional objective. It is also helpful to have

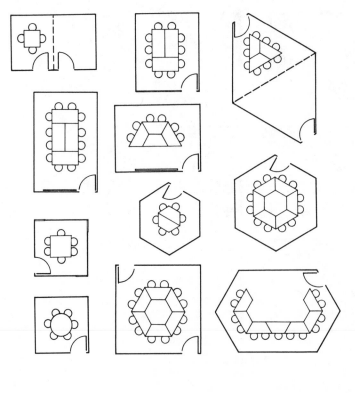

FIG. 1-5 *Small-group activity arrangements (courtesy Educational Facilities Laboratories and The School Library)*

an inventory list of the contents of each box so the children can report missing items to you immediately.

3. Have basic materials—pencils, erasers, and paper—on hand at the appropriate centers at the beginning of each day.

4. Teach the children to clean up after themselves.

5. Hold the children responsible for the materials they check out from shelf and supply areas. They should take the responsibility for keeping these areas in order.

6. Teach the children to take inventory and report damaged or missing items to you. Check sheets devised for this purpose can be posted at each center and beside shelves and cabinets.

7. Have containers for holding materials and supplies available at each center.

Teacher-made Materials Containers

In exchange for a little time and a little ingenuity, resourceful teachers can make a variety of colorful, durable materials containers that are fun and easy for children to use. The following items can be stored in teacher-made containers:

Pencils, erasers, crayons. Small paper or metal juice cans make excellent pencil holders. Tape the exposed edges, then cover the cans with adhesive shelf paper.

Books. Cut corrugated cardboard boxes to size and reinforce the edges with tape. Use them for storing library books, workbooks, and other packaged materials.

Paints, paste. Plastic chip dip containers with lids are ideal for storing these art materials, as well as for holding paper clips, tacks, pins, and other small fasteners.

Paint brushes, scissors, small rulers. Coffee cans covered with adhesive shelf paper make sturdy, stable containers. Cover the exposed edges if they are rough or sharp.

Workbook holders. Cover large ice cream cartons with lined paper to make labeling them easy, or cover them with construction paper for color-code identification. A symbol—leaf, star, or car—may be used to identify materials to be used by a specific group.

Filmstrip containers. Egg cartons make handy storage units for filmstrips. One egg carton can hold a dozen filmstrip cans; label each place with the catalog number of the filmstrip. In the primary grades, color coding or symbols can be used instead of numerals to help children locate and replace the filmstrips.

Ditto work sheets. Ditto materials made with spirit duplicators can be stored in appropriately labeled ditto master boxes.

Miscellaneous materials. The bottom halves of plastic bleach jugs can be used for a variety of storage purposes. Cut off the tops with a knife, then tape the edges. Tacks, pins, and other small items can be stored in egg cartons.

Concluding Thoughts

You have now been introduced to a variety of general ideas that may help you modify your classroom for the use of learning centers. As your centers take shape, pay special attention to developing student responsibility for learning, noise control, and movement among the centers.

1. *Students should take the responsibility for their own learning*, both in team and independent activities. As a member of a team, each student is to carry his own load, control his behavior so that he does not interfere with others, and complete, check, and file his own work. In addition, each student should help the others control their behavior so that the learning center concept continues to work successfully.

2. *The noise level should be controlled to meet standards set by the students*. Each teacher and each child has his own noise tolerance level. If the room is too noisy, many children will not be able to work satisfactorily. Discuss with the children the amount of noise that will be tolerated, then devise signals that will tell them when it is too noisy. A whistle, bell, or flick of the light switch are signals all will notice. A busy classroom will have a hum of constructive noise. Neither absolute silence nor complete abandon is desirable.

3. *Movement in the classroom should be controlled to meet standards set by the students*. Room arrangement is an important consideration here. Pathways to and from learning centers, the drinking fountain, pencil sharpeners, and storage areas should all be planned carefully. In addition, behavior guidelines such as prohibitions on running, shoving, and pushing, should be developed in discussions with the children in order to maintain standards of safety and to help avoid confusion.

If a child cannot control his own behavior, develop alternatives to learning center activities for him. At first he may be suspended from center activities for a time, but if his behavior continues to be disruptive, it may indicate that the child is not ready for center activities and should be placed in a more structured program.

Selected References

Bloom, Benjamin S., ed. *Taxonomy of Educational Objectives*. New York: David McKay Company, 1956.

Ellsworth, Ralph E. *The School Library: Facilities for Independent Study in the Secondary School*. New York: Educational Facilities Laboratories, 1968.

Howes, Virgil M. *Individualization of Instruction: A Teaching Strategy*. New York: The Macmillan Co., 1970.

Kemp, Jerrold E. *Instructional Design*. Belmont, Calif.: Fearon Publishers/Lear Siegler, Inc., 1971.

Kibler, Baker, and Miles. *Behavioral Objectives and In-struction*. Boston: Allyn and Bacon, Inc., 1970.

Mager, Robert F. *Developing Vocational Instruction*. Belmont, Calif.: Fearon Publishers, 1967.

Mager, Robert F. *Preparing Instructional Objectives*. Belmont, Calif.: Fearon Publishers, 1962.

Popham, James, and Eva Baker: *Planning an Instructional Sequence*. Englewood Cliffs, N.J.: Prentice-Hall, 1970.

Popham, James, and Eva Baker. *Systematic Instruction*. Englewood Cliffs, N.J.: Prentice-Hall, 1970.

Skinner, B. F. *The Technology of Teaching*. New York: Appleton-Century-Crofts, 1968.

Wadsworth, Barry J. *Piaget's Theory of Cognitive De-velopment*. New York: David McKay Company, 1971.

Teacher-prepared Materials and Equipment

TODAY'S teachers can select classroom materials from a wide range of commercially prepared items. However, when funds are lacking or when commercial materials do not meet the needs of children in a specific learning situation, teachers may need to prepare their own materials. In some instances, a classroom teacher might use multi-media packages incorporating such materials as audio tapes, records, filmstrips, and pictures. In other situations, a box of ditto worksheets may be central to learning center activities. Colorful self-adhesive shelf paper can help the teacher turn a discarded cardboard carton or coffee can into a highly motivational, useful learning device. Inexpensive electronic parts and the assistance of persons with simple electronic skills can provide the teacher with highly creative learning devices at minimal cost.

The teacher needs to know which materials are best suited to the objectives of the lesson, how to select them, and how to make them. Several items of general interest which have found favor with teachers and have been successful in classroom work are presented here. Suggestions for the use of selected audiovisual media are also included. Specific applications of these and other items, as well as a discussion of commercially available materials, are presented in Section II.

MANIPULATIVE-DRILL MATERIALS

Children should be encouraged to discover basic concepts on their own through manipulation and experimentation. Commercial organizations and publishers have recently given new emphasis to the development of materials, useful at all grade levels, for learning through a variety of personal, firsthand experiences. In order to be of maximum use, learning center materials must provide the children with immediate feedback on their performance. Materials can be color-coded, keyed by size or shape, or programmed in some other way to indicate to the child that he is learning.

Electric Response Boards

The electric response board can be used to develop:

Hand and Eye Coordination. The board can be used in early childhood education to teach shapes, colors, and symbols. For example, the children can match shapes that appear on both sides of the board.

Right and Left Hand Discrimination. The teacher can name an object on the left side of the board and ask the student to select that object using his left hand. The teacher can then name an object on the right side of the board and have the student select it using his right hand.

Dexterity and Coordination. The students can use both hands simultaneously to perform a learning task.

Motivation. The board requires personal involvement and provides immediate feedback. Learning becomes more like a game.

Independent Study. The student can work alone at his own pace, learning, reviewing, and testing himself.

The electric response board is an excellent all-around learning tool that can be used with many age groups and in many subject areas. Students enjoy working with the board, and social interaction is stimulated through mutual interest and competition in solving the problems it presents. The board is easy to construct and can be made with tools usually available in the home or school.

BASIC THEORY

A basic type of electric response board, shown in Fig. 2-1, works on the simple series circuit theory. When probe A touches one end of the circuit wire attached to the *number* four, and probe B touches the other end of the circuit wire attached to the *word* four, the circuit is complete. Electricity can then flow from the cell, through the lamp, through the connecting wire, and back to the cell. When the lamp lights up, the student knows he has chosen the correct answer.

Various adaptations of this basic board can be devised. More question-answer terminals can be added, or the question-answer card can be divided so that one card always asks the same question, but several other cards can be used interchangeably for the answers. For example, Fig. 2-1 shows the questions as numbers and the answers as words but the answers also could be Roman numerals, tally marks, clock faces, or words in foreign languages. Other types of electric response boards are described in this chapter, but this version is the easiest one to construct.

UNDERSTANDING THE PARTS

The most complete source of materials is your local electronic supply house, where help in selecting materials is usually available. Hardware and variety stores are also useful, depending on the complexity of the board.

Dry cells are available in various sizes, but all sizes produce 1½ volts of electricity. The bigger the cell, the longer it will last. Standard flashlight cells, size D, are adequate for electric response boards.

For best results, the connecting wires should be securely fastened to the cell. Solder the wire to the cell, use a cell holder (which also allows you to change the cell easily), or simply tape the wire to the cell. Taping is the least desirable method because the wires can easily come loose.

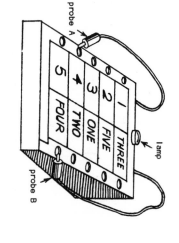

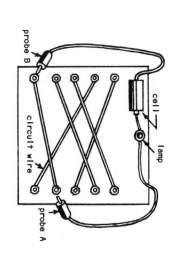

Fig. 2-1 *Electric response board (top and bottom views)*

Nine-volt transistor radio batteries are also useful. The transistor radio battery clip, sold as a separate item, attaches securely to the battery.

The lamp should have the same voltage as the cell it will be used with. Wires can be soldered directly to the lamp or lamp socket. Some lamps are available with the wires permanently attached for simplified installation and connection.

Round-headed machine screws and machine screw nuts make good question-answer terminals and program wire fasteners. Size 6/32 is recommended, although any type or size will work.

Paper fasteners can be used as question-answer terminals and are especially useful if alligator clip leads are used for program wires.

Wire comes in many sizes and colors. It is sized by number. The bigger the number, the smaller the wire, so a size 20 wire would be half as thick as a size 10 wire. Number 24 plastic-coated, stranded copper wire is a good size for electric response boards.

The probe is the part the student holds. It is simply a convenience, not essential but recommended.

Alligator clip leads are available individually or in packages of ten. Each lead usually consists of two alligator clips connected to either end of a wire that is about fifteen inches long. These leads are both inexpensive and easy to use. They eliminate the need for soldering and facilitate programming.

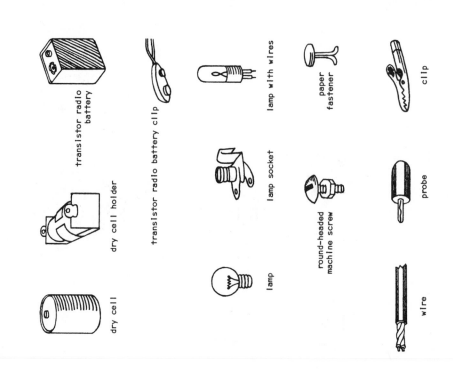

dry cell

dry cell holder

transistor radio battery

transistor radio battery clip

lamp

lamp socket

lamp with wires

round-headed machine screw

paper fastener

wire

probe

clip

When designing your electric response board, consider the following points:

1. Allow for easy changing of the answer sequence.
2. Allow for easy changing of question-answer cards.
3. Should question and answer cards be separate? This design feature would allow for greater flexibility in programming.
4. Who will use the board? How durable should it be? (Should you use plywood or cardboard?) How should you decorate it?
5. Could the students make their own programs?
6. Do you have soldering facilities?

Standard/Display Program

This board provides for a standard program or a program that works in conjunction with attached charts, drawings, or pictures. On the standard program, the questions are on one side and the answers are on the other side of the same program.

The display program uses a standard board with an attached sheet of information. For the board in Fig. 2-2, "Identify Major California Cities," a map of California with numbers covering selected city names is placed in the display holder. The names of the cities are listed on the left side of the board, and the numbers that correspond to those cities are listed on the right. The student touches one probe to a city name, locates that city on the

FIG. 2-2 *Standard/display program*

map, then touches the other probe to the corresponding number on the program. If both parts of the response are correct, the circuit will be completed and the light will flash.

Flexible Program

On this board, one half of the program can be changed independently of the other half. For example, the left side could be numbered one through ten and the right side could alternately show the words one through ten, Roman numerals, clock faces showing time, or numbers written in Spanish (Fig. 2-3).

MATERIALS:
- 1 transistor radio battery, 9 volts
- 2 alligator clip leads
- lamp and reflector
- standard transistor radio battery connector
- two probes
- paper fasteners or round-headed machine screws
- plastic-coated, stranded copper wire, #24, 4 feet
- contact cement
- tape, 1 or 1½ inches wide
- mat knife
- drill or nail

CONSTRUCTION: Except for the method of programming, the construction of these two boards is the same. Draw Fig. 2-4 to full size on mat board or any other desired

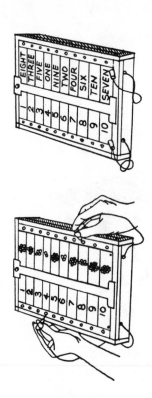

FIG. 2-3 *Flexible program*

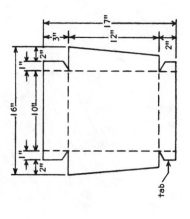

FIG. 2-4 *Diagram of standard/display or flexible program*

material. Mat board is handy because it can be cut and formed easily with simple tools and is available in a variety of colors.

Cut along the solid lines and score the board from the top along the dashed lines. Make holes for the question-answer terminals and probe wires using a nail or a drill. Make a hole for the lamp. Fold the board along the dashed lines until it is the proper shape.

Glue the tabs down to hold it together. Glue on the program holders.

Install the hardware, as shown in Fig. 2-1. Wire the board, then trim it with cloth or plastic tape as reinforcement and decoration.

Fig. 2-2 shows a display holder and Fig. 2-3 shows a flexible holder. Although many teachers find program holders useful, they are not always essential. For the display program, lay the display on the table. For the flexible program, use a left and a right card.

CIRCUIT: To program the board, attach one end of the wire to a question terminal and the other end to the corresponding answer terminal, as shown in Fig. 2-1.

COST: $3–$4.

Circuit Board

This type of electric response board (Fig. 2-5) is the easiest to make. Each program has its own circuit, so the board does not have to be reprogrammed.

FIG. 2-5 *Circuit board*

MATERIALS:
- mat board or heavy cardboard
- plastic-coated, stranded copper wire, #24, 4 feet
- lamp
- aluminum self-adhesive tape or aluminum foil
- paper fasteners
- dry cell(s)
- glue
- solder iron
- mat knife

CONSTRUCTION: Cut the board to size as shown in Fig. 2-6. Fold it along the dotted lines. Tie a knot in each wire so it does not pull through the board (Fig. 2-7). Fasten the battery to the board with glue or tape. Cut out a hole for the lamp just large enough for the lamp to fit in snugly. Glue the lamp in place if necessary. The lead wire should be long enough to reach easily to all question-answer terminals. The probes in Fig. 2-5 are paper fasteners soldered to lead wires. A transistor radio battery and lamp can be used to eliminate soldering. Program the board with a list of questions and answers (Fig. 2-8).

CIRCUIT: Connect question-answer terminals with self-adhesive aluminum tape, or glue strips of aluminum foil between them (Fig. 2-9). Where two pieces of aluminum cross, separate them with transparent tape. Cover the circuits with cardboard or contact paper for protection.

COST: Approximately $.50.

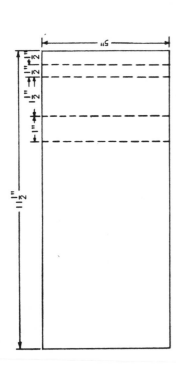

FIG. 2-6 *Diagram of circuit board*

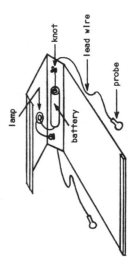

FIG. 2-7 *Circuit board (assembled)*

Independent Study Devices

Independent study devices can be made inexpensively from materials usually available at school. The cost of these boards—about two cents each—allows the students to keep as well as make their own learning devices.

The teacher designs the basic shape and provides the students with copies or a method of copying it (such as a template to trace around). The students cut out, color, and program their own devices.

The design and complexity of the program depend on the student's ability. Individual programming allows each student to learn what he decides he needs to learn. The process of making the program is a learning experience in itself. When designed to fit into a shirt pocket, slip boards provide the student with a personal method of learning, available when he needs it, and programmed to teach him what he wants to learn.

In general, these independent study devices provide immediate feedback, motivation, student involvement, and personal learning.

Slip Board

MATERIALS:
- construction paper
- ditto paper
- glue
- tape
- modeling knife or razor blade
- scissors
- stapler

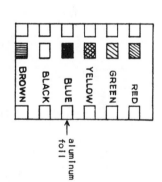

FIG. 2-8 *Circuit board program (top view)*

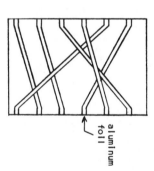

FIG. 2-9 *Circuit board program (bottom view)*

CONSTRUCTION: Ditto the outline on construction paper as shown in Fig. 2-11. Cut out the program holder. Fold it as illustrated and fasten it in back with tape, glue, or staples. Let the students decorate their own slip boards.

The program in Fig. 2-11 was made on 8½" × 11" ditto paper folded in sixths to make twelve programs. To program the slip board, write a problem on the left side, then pull up the program until the problem disappears and write the answer on the right side.

OTHER CONSIDERATIONS: Boards can be made in various sizes, but the standard sizes of available materials should be considered. Ditto paper is 8½" × 11" and standard construction paper is 9" × 12".

Dial Board

MATERIALS:
- heavy paper
- paper fasteners
- color crayons
- heavy cardboard
- scissors
- modeling knife or razor blade

CONSTRUCTION: Copy the pattern in Fig. 2-12 on a piece of construction paper. Cut out the pieces and join them in the center with a paper fastener. Write directly on the program with a felt pen or other marker. Write the problem and the answer, then move the program until a blank area appears and repeat.

FIG. 2-10 *Independent study devices*

OTHER CONSIDERATIONS: Use one of the designs shown here, or create your own. Make patterns out of heavy cardboard, then let the students trace around them and cut out their own boards. The size of the board depends on the level of the student.

Peek Board

MATERIALS:
- heavy cardboard
- tape
- glue
- modeling knife or razor blade
- ruler
- color markers

CONSTRUCTION: Cut two pieces of heavy cardboard to the desired size. Cut doors and reinforce them with tape from the back, as shown in Fig. 2-13. Glue top piece to bottom piece at the edges.

Write a question or problem on each door, then write the answers under the doors. Let the children color or decorate their boards as appropriate. Other kinds of peek boards are shown in Fig. 2-14.

Self-instructional Puzzles

Children can be taught numerous concepts through the use of self-instructional puzzles. The examples presented here illustrate only a few of the possibilities. The puzzles are suitable for a variety of subjects and grade levels.

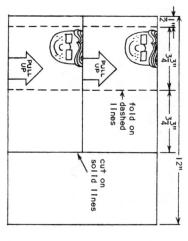

tape or staple or glue

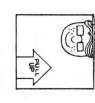

Fig. 2-11 *Slip board*

TWO TABLE	FOUR TABLE	FIVE TABLE
2 x 1 = 2		
2 x 2 = 4		
2 x 3 = 6		
2 x 4 = 8		
2 x 5 = 10		
2 x 6 = 12		
2 x 7 = 14		

THREE TABLE	SIX TABLE	SEVEN TABLE

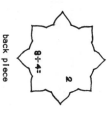

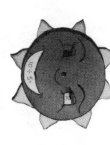

8 ÷ 4 =

2

back piece

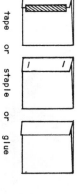

front piece

Fig. 2-12 *Dial board*

MATERIALS: · pictures
· felt pen
· laminating plastic or transparent shelf paper
· heavy cardboard
· glue
· paper cutter
· mat knife or razor blade

CONSTRUCTION: Glue a picture on the cardboard, or draw a picture on it as desired. Laminate the cardboard with plastic or transparent shelf paper.[1] Cut the laminated pictures into pieces using diagonal or curved strokes that vary with each cut.

OTHER CONSIDERATIONS: Puzzles can also be used for teaching word and letter recognition. Children's coloring books, the Sunday comics, and magazine advertisements will give you other useful ideas.

The puzzle in Fig. 2-15 shows how skills of counting and numeral and word recognition can be combined in one puzzle. Note how the cuts vary so the puzzle can be completed in one sequence only. When making several puzzles cut them from cardboard of different sizes so the pieces cannot be confused. Add lines or frames around the illustrations as additional clues (see Figs. 16 and 17).

[1]Complete directions for mounting and laminating are found in John E. Morlan, *Preparation of Inexpensive Teaching Materials* (New York: Intext, Chandler Publishing Company, 1973).

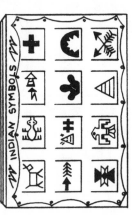

FIG. 2-13 *Peek board (parts)*

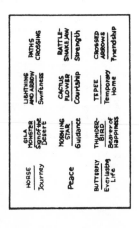

FIG. 2-14 *Peek boards (assembled)*

Lift sign for answer.

Lift door for answer.

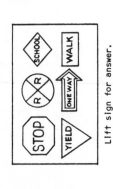

Each feather is different color. Correct answer is behind each feather.

Construction paper colors are attached to palette. Lift color for answer.

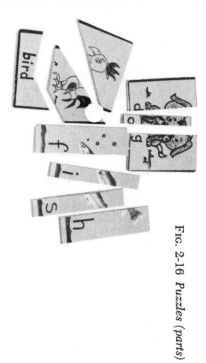

FIG. 2-16 *Puzzles (parts)*

FIG. 2-15 *Math puzzle*

FIG. 2-17 *Puzzles (assembled)*

Store puzzles in envelopes or plastic bags labeled appropriately. Keep them in one place and teach the children to put them away when they have finished working with them.

Display Devices

Teachers who use classroom learning centers encounter a wide range of problems involving the display of learning materials. They need to display materials that give directions, ask questions, present problems, and provide information. Often, these materials must be displayed using a minimum of tabletop work space. Some teachers solve this problem by arranging learning centers on tables in front of bulletin boards and tacking materials to the board. This system works well for some, but not all, projects. Other display devices that have proven to be particularly successful are the accordion-fold display set, the individual visograph display, the accordion-fold visograph display, the chart visograph, and the pocket chart.

Accordion-fold Display Set

It is often necessary to display a series of pictures beside an arrangement of realia or printed materials. An eye-catching display can be made using pressure-sensitive tape to fasten a series of prints or illustrations together in an attractive arrangement that can be folded for easy storage (Fig. 2-18).

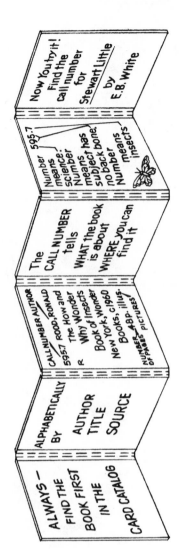

FIG. 2-18 *Accordion-fold display set*

MATERIALS: • pictures
• tape (cloth, plastic, or masking)
• scissors

CONSTRUCTION: Place the pictures face down on a clean surface in the desired sequence. Tape the materials together, leaving an ⅛-inch space between the pictures. Turn the set over and tape the other side, covering the spaces between illustrations. If materials of varying heights are used, the bottom edges should be aligned, but the top can be uneven.

Fold the display set along the taped edges, then set it up. The accordion-fold display set is especially useful as a reference device and for giving step-by-step directions.

Individual Visograph

The individual visograph, featuring a reusable plastic working surface, can be used for displaying flat graphic materials. Pictures or selected illustrations can be slipped under the plastic covering. The visograph can be tacked on a bulletin board or placed on a stand (Fig. 2-19).

The visograph also makes an ideal work-study device because it has a reusable working surface. If you slip a worksheet under the plastic and have a child mark on the see-through plastic with a grease pencil or water-soluble felt marker, he can practice skills or test himself. Do not use waxed crayons or permanent inks because they will damage the plastic.

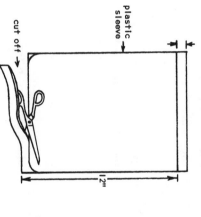

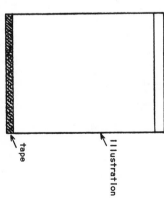

2. Pull on plastic sleeve. Cut off bottom.

plastic sleeve

cut off

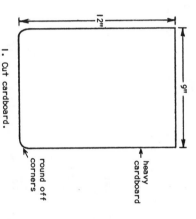

1. Cut cardboard.

12"

9"

heavy cardboard

round off corners

3. Finished visograph.

12"

tape

Illustration

FIG. 2-19 *Individual visograph*

After a child has marked his answer, he can check his work immediately using an answer key, or ask the teacher to check it for him. The visograph can be erased easily with a soft cloth and used by another child. In this manner, one worksheet can be used a number of times by a number of children because no one marks directly on the paper.

MATERIALS: • cardboard 9" × 12"
• plastic sleeve 9" × 12" (cost is less than 3¢ per bag)[2]
• tape (cloth, plastic, or masking)
• scissors

CONSTRUCTION: Cut the cardboard to size (19" × 12"). Use heavy cardboard for strength and stability. Round off the two bottom corners so they will not tear the sleeve as you pull it on. Pull the plastic bag over the cardboard until it is one inch from the top. Cut off the bottom of the bag as illustrated, then tape the bottom of the visograph closed. Be sure that the tape touches both the plastic and the cardboard on each side so the plastic will not slip.

OTHER CONSIDERATIONS: If the visograph is covered on both sides by a plastic sleeve, a worksheet can be slipped into one side and the answer sheet inserted in the back.

When used as a work-study device, the visograph can be programmed with questions and answers and laid flat on a table, ready to use, with a grease pencil beside it. If the visograph is to be used as a display device, only one side needs to be covered with plastic.

Accordion-fold Visograph Display

This device combines the advantages of both the accordion-fold display set and the individual visograph. It is particularly useful for displaying directions in a sequence or for a series of related materials. The accordion-fold visograph stands on any flat surface and takes up little work space. The materials can be changed quickly and easily, and the display folds up compactly for storage.

MATERIALS: • cardboard
• plastic sheets or plastic sleeves
• scissors
• paper cutter
• tape

CONSTRUCTION: Cut three cardboard sheets to the same size. Cut two plastic sheets 1 inch shorter and the same width as the cardboard sheets. The plastic pockets on the right can be made any size desired (Fig. 2-20).

Tape the plastic sheets to the cardboard as illustrated, leaving the tape edge open. Tape the plastic pockets in place on the third piece of cardboard.

[2]Dorfman Products, 23813 Archwood Street, Canoga Park, CA 91304.

Align the three pieces of cardboard, then tape them together, leaving a ¼-inch space between the pieces. Turn the set over and tape the other side, covering the spaces between the cardboard. Insert the illustrations as shown in Fig. 2-20.

Chart Visograph

The chart visograph is an enlarged version of the individual visograph, with only minor modifications in construction details. It is especially useful for displaying large graphic materials such as maps and charts. Because the working surface is plastic, the children can mark on it with grease pencil or water-soluble ink pens. Students can use this type of visograph to outline maps, complete stories, correct punctuation, or solve problems, leaving the original materials untouched.

MATERIALS:
- cardboard
- plastic or acetate sheet
- tape
- rubber cement or other adhesive

CONSTRUCTION: Cut the cardboard to size. Cut the plastic sheet about 1 inch shorter than the cardboard, but the same width. Cut three narrow ⅛"–¼" cardboard strips. Two of the strips should be cut ¼ inch shorter than the length of the plastic sheet, and one strip should be cut the same length as the width of the plastic sheet. Glue this strip to the bottom edge of the cardboard, and glue the other two strips to the side edges of the cardboard.

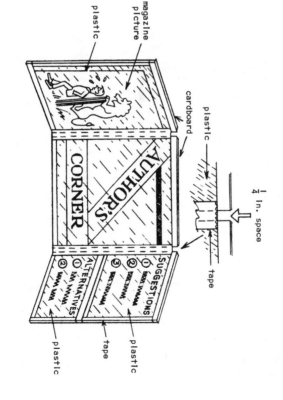

FIG. 2-20 Accordion-fold visograph display

Tape the top edge of the plastic sheet. This will protect the user from cutting himself on the pastic as the display material is inserted or removed.

Tape the plastic sheet to the cardboard strips, making sure that the tape is pulled around to the back of the cardboard for added strength. You may wish to fasten a cardboard hinge on the back of the cardboard to serve as a stand (Fig. 2-21).

Pocket Charts

The problems of flexible scheduling created by the use of classroom learning centers can be solved in part by the use of pocket charts. An assignment chart can be used to hold student name cards or to indicate various activity groups. An instructional chart can be used to display words, pictures, or materials.

Instructional Pocket Chart

MATERIALS: • cardboard (medium to heavy weight)
• tagboard (light weight)
• tape
• paper cutter or scissors
• ruler

CONSTRUCTION: Cut the cardboard to the desired size. Cut three strips of lightweight tagboard as long as the cardboard sheet is wide. (Cardboard can also be used for these strips). Cut the strips at least 3 inches wide. Fold

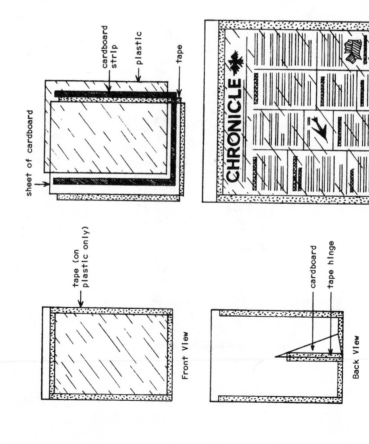

FIG. 2-21 *Chart visograph*

them as illustrated in Fig. 2-22, and tape them in place on the cardboard sheet along the top edge of the strip. Repeat these steps for each pocket.

Fold the strips up and tape the bottom edge of each pocket to the cardboard sheet. Hold the tagboard pocket firmly against the cardboard and tape the ends of each pocket closed as shown. The finished pockets are then ready to be used.

Assignment Pocket Chart

MATERIALS: • library card pockets, one for each learning center
• cardboard (medium to heavy weight)
• rubber cement or white glue
• clear adhesive shelf paper
• scissors
• razor blade
• pencil

CONSTRUCTION: Cut the cardboard to size. Arrange the pockets and mark their positions with a pencil. Glue them in place.

Cover the chart with clear adhesive shelf paper. Cut openings at the top of the pockets. Insert name cards or use pictures for primary and preschool children.

If you plan to label or decorate the chart, be sure to do so before laminating it. Symbols or pictures can be used on the pockets to indicate the learning centers they represent (Fig. 2-23).

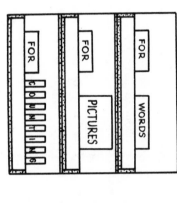

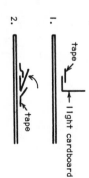

FIG. 2-22 *Instructional Pocket Chart*

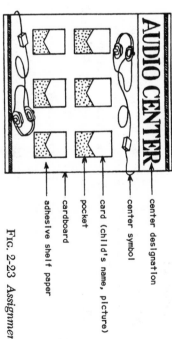

FIG. 2-23 *Assignment Pocket Chart*

Projection-Viewing Materials

Projected materials are central to many classroom learning activities. Commercial filmstrip viewers are useful tools for independent study, and filmstrip, slide, and 8mm loop projectors all have a place in group work. The wide variety of inexpensive projectors now on the market makes it possible for every classroom to have its own projection center. It is essential to use reflected projection screens or daylight screens if the projections are to be successful in a lighted room. These may be purchased from a commercial firm or made by the teacher for less than one dollar each.

THINGS TO CONSIDER

In addition to choosing appropriate films, slides, and filmstrips and using the appropriate projectors and screens, special consideration should be given to the following points:

1. *Give the children thorough instructions on how to use the equipment.* Plug in the equipment yourself to avoid the danger of electrical shock to the children. Place power cords out of the way so children will not trip over them.

2. *Learn how to change the projection bulb on each machine you use.* Have spare bulbs available in case one burns out. Remember to unplug the equipment before changing bulbs.

3. *Position the screen so that light from windows will not fall directly on it.* To ensure a bright image, place the screen parallel to the row of windows or project the film at an angle toward the windows.

4. *Make the children responsible for all materials used at the center.* A check-out and inventory system, and a system of reporting damaged or missing materials will help the program run smoothly.

5. *Teach the children to handle slides and filmstrips by the edges* to avoid damaging the pictures. If the strips are not in cartridges, teach the children how to reroll them properly. Projection materials should always be returned to their proper places after use. Checklists or charts can serve as reminders.

6. *Mark the placement of projectors, viewers, and screens on the table.* Use tape to label the equipment and to outline the place where each piece should stand. Color coding may help. (A filmstrip projector marked with blue, for example, stands on a blue label, and an individual viewer marked with red stands on a red label.) If permissible, use felt pens to mark the outline of projection and viewing equipment directly on the table. It is especially useful to indicate placement when the projection equipment must be moved frequently to permit other activities at the same center. Before removing burned-out projection bulbs, unplug the

7. *Take every precaution to ensure student safety.* Before removing burned-out projection bulbs, unplug the machine and allow it to cool. Check frequently for frayed cords. If possible, use three-pronged plugs to avoid possible electric shocks.

8. *Be sure to provide for feedback from the viewing experience* through follow-up or concomitant activities, such as creative writing, research in related literature, study of programmed review materials, or work with a study guide.

9. *Students can benefit from the use of study guide sheets* which ask questions they can answer while viewing the related material. Follow-up activities and new vocabulary terms can be included on the sheet. By checking through the student responses, you can find out whether or not the child is learning and meeting the objectives of the viewing experience.

Teacher-made Projection Screens

There are many daylight screens and rear projection screens on the market that are suitable for use in classroom learning centers. In cases where school budgets are already severely strained, however, it may not be possible to purchase them. For little expense, teachers can make screens which are as efficient and as useful as expensive commercial models.

Cardboard Carton Daylight Screen

If it is set up on a table at least three feet long, the daylight screen works well for all kinds of projected materials. Because the finished screen is a modified box, only a minimum amount of light reaches the projection

surface inside and a brilliant image can be seen even in a fully lighted room. The box is modified so that the sides slant inward, providing a line-of-sight viewing angle that is suitable for small group work at a learning center. In most instances, the screen can be made with items available in the school supply room. This screen can easily be constructed in an hour or less, once the needed materials have been assembled.

MATERIALS:
- cardboard carton longer than it is wide
- packaging or masking tape
- glue
- knife or single-edge razor blade
- black paint (flat enamel or tempera)
- shelf paper
- ruler

CONSTRUCTION: Cut off the flaps of the cardboard box and place it on a table as shown in Fig. 2-24. (A ditto-paper carton, available at most schools, was used here.) Using a ruler, draw diagonal lines in pencil across the top of the box from the corners of the open end to a point about 3½ inches from each side. The angle at which you mark the lines will determine the viewing angle (line of sight) of the finished screen. It may be altered to suit your individual needs. Turn the carton over, and draw two lines on the other side at the same angle.

Turn the carton around so that the back (originally the bottom) of the carton is toward you. Connect the diagonal lines on top and bottom with two vertical lines as shown. Cut the diagonal lines all the way through the

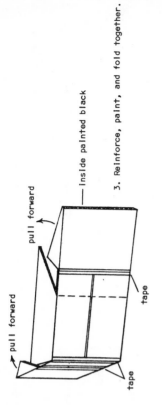

FRONT VIEW

diagonal lines

top

3½"   18"   3½"

12"

10"

remove flaps

cardboard carton

remove flaps

1. Remove flaps and draw diagonal lines.

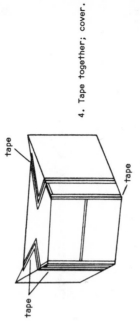

pull forward

pull forward

pull forward

Inside painted black

tape

tape

3. Reinforce, paint, and fold together.

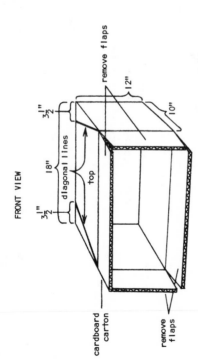

BACK VIEW

side

top

12"

3½"

score

11"

cut (both top and bottom)

2. Draw vertical lines on the back; cut and score.

tape

tape

tape

4. Tape together; cover.

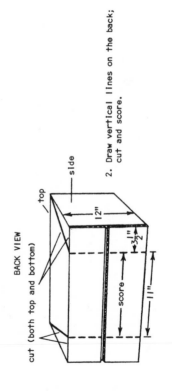

adhesive shelf paper

white cardboard

tape

5. Finished screen.

FIG. 2-24 *Cardboard carton daylight screen*

cardboard, then cut along the back toward the sides as illustrated. Cut halfway through the cardboard along the vertical lines. Then turn the box over and cut the bottom as you did the top.

Pull both sides straight back and reinforce them with tape as illustrated. Paint the inside of the box black, and let it dry.

Pull the sides of the box all the way forward from the scored lines, then tape them to the top and bottom. For added strength, glue strips of overlapping cardboard along the seams.

Tape a piece of white cardboard inside the box to serve as the projection surface. Railroad board works well. To add a decorative touch, cover the box with adhesive shelf paper. The screen is now ready to use.

This screen may be used for filmstrips, slides, and motion pictures. To raise or lower the screen, stand it on books or blocks of the appropriate height.

Cardboard Carton Reflected Projection Screen

Using this device, the projector can be placed very close to the screen and still produce a large image. The viewing angle for this type of screen is greater than for a daylight screen because no shading is necessary at the top or at the sides. Construction of this screen is a bit more expensive and time-consuming than for the daylight model, but the finished product is well worth the additional money and effort. The reflected projection screen can be used with slide, filmstrip and 8mm or 16mm picture projectors (Fig. 2-25).

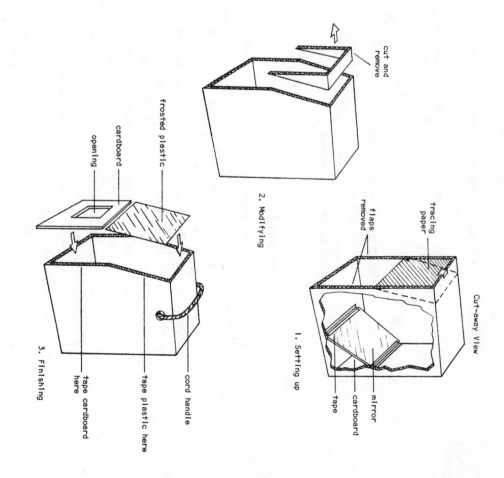

FIG. 2-25 *Cardboard carton reflected projection screen*

MATERIALS: · cardboard carton longer than it is wide (it should be at least 12 inches wide)
· mirror (mirror tile available at hardware stores is fine)
· tracing paper
· tape
· sharp modeling knife or razor blade
· heavyweight frosted plastic or diffusion plastic (white paper or sailcloth may be substituted if necessary)
· glue
· black paint
· nylon cord

CONSTRUCTION: Cut the flaps off the box. Glue the mirror to the center of a piece of cardboard slightly longer than the mirror and just as wide. Place the mirror inside the box at an angle so it tilts slightly as illustrated. Temporarily tape a piece of tracing paper over the top half of the open end of the box as shown. Project a slide or filmstrip into the box. Adjust the position of the mirror until the image appears framed on the tracing paper. Tape it in place. Move the projector backward or forward until the size of the image is correct. The image will be wider at the top than at the bottom. To eliminate this distortion, pull the bottom end of the tracing paper away from the box until the sides of the image are parallel. Note the angle at which you are holding the paper and mark it on the box, as illustrated. Cut off the cardboard wedge at the top. Paint the inside of the box.

Cut a piece of frosted plastic or diffusion plastic that fits over the open end where the wedge was cut off. Tape it to the box. (If plastic is not available, white paper or sailcloth can be substituted as a screen surface. The projected image, however, will not be quite as sharp.)

Cut a piece of cardboard large enough to cover the remaining opening. Project a picture into the box and adjust the image to the proper size. Place the cut cardboard against the box. Note the area covered by the projected light and mark the area with a pencil. Using the pencil marks as guidelines, cut a square opening ½ inch larger than the marks on all sides. Tape the cardboard to the box and add a nylon cord handle if desired. Paint the box or cover it with adhesive shelf paper.

The reflected projection screen looks much like a television screen. It works well in a lighted room and has an exceptionally wide viewing angle. Because a large image is reflected even when the projector is set close to the box, this screen can be set up on a small table.

Audio Learning Center Materials

The audio learning center is useful in virtually every subject area for giving directions to students on how to proceed with observation, experimentation, or other activities. It may also serve as a source of materials for drill and practice, for listening activities, and for creative writing. The application of audio center activities to various subject areas is treated more fully in Section II.

THINGS TO CONSIDER

Most audio learning centers are equipped with a tape recorder, and some use disc playback or record player equipment as well. In order to ensure that the audio equipment does not interfere with other activities in the room, it is essential to provide earphones. Selection of playback equipment, recording equipment, earphones, and the distribution system are all of major importance.

1. *Select tape recorders that are easy to operate and maintain.* Cassette recorders are especially useful. Be sure the ones you choose have capstan drive, are easy to load and unload, and are powered by AC-DC current. In the long run battery operation may become prohibitively expensive for the teacher or the school. Be sure that the tape recorders you select have a good guarantee, and that they can be repaired locally. Monoaural recorders are satisfactory for most classroom purposes.

2. *Select earphones that match your recorder.* Wattage output and the size of the connecting plugs and receptacles are very important. Choose only those which are well constructed and durable. It is a good idea to check on earphones when you purchase your tape recorders. Some schools have purchased recorders and earphones separately, only to find they do not work satisfactorily in the classroom.

3. *Select or construct an appropriate sound distribution system.* There are several satisfactory sound distribution systems on the market. Consult the Selected References at the end of this chapter for specific suggestions. (A discussion of the basic electronic components is included in Chapter 3.)

4. *Locate the audio center near an electrical outlet* so all power cords will be out of the way. Do not string them where children can trip on them.

5. *Provide carrels for individual work* if you plan to use the audio center for drill activities. This arrangement is particularly helpful in eliminating distractions when audio card readers such as the Language Master[3] are used.

6. *Select a seating arrangement that meets the needs of your group.* Fig. 2-26 may give you some ideas as you design your own center. It is best to install cords and outlets for earphones around the edge of the table. This way, the hardware takes up no table space, though it is more expensive to install this arrangement than to use a jackbox in the center of the table. If table space is not available for use as an audio center, a floor area may be used.

STORAGE

Be sure to arrange for the proper storage of tapes, records, and other materials used in the audio center.

[3]Language Master, Bell and Howell Company, 7100 McCormick Road, Chicago, IL 60645

1. *Prepare and label a box for storing earphones and other audio equipment.* A cardboard box covered with adhesive shelf paper makes a simple, readily identifiable container. Teach the children to roll up their earphone cords and fasten them with rubber bands at the end of the lesson.

2. *Store tapes near the other materials needed to complete the audio lesson*—realia, worksheets, or manipulative materials. When storing materials of assorted media in the same box, it is best to post a list of the contents nearby for inventory purposes. If the tapes must be stored separately, it is essential to devise a cross-reference system between the tape box and the other materials.

3. *Store records vertically in a rack.* Cross-reference them with the other materials.

LESSON PLANNING AND PROCEDURES

Follow the suggestions for lesson development presented in Chapter 1. After you have listed your objectives —what you want the students to be able to do, know, and understand—list the activities and materials that will help them achieve the objectives. Plan a record-keeping system and a feedback system that lets the students know how well they are progressing. Next, you are ready to make the tape.

1. *Collect the materials you have listed and write a preliminary script of what you want to say on the tape.* Have a fellow teacher listen to it and offer suggestions.

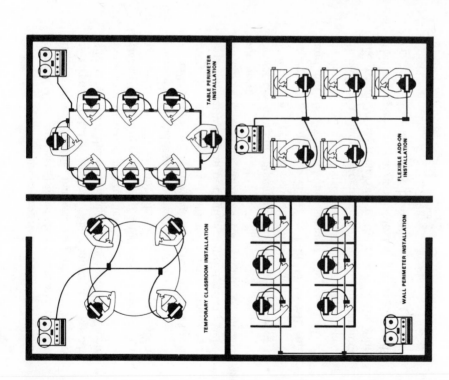

Fig. 2-26 *Suggested sound distribution arrangements (courtesy TELEX systems)*

2. *Use these materials in a trial lesson with a student of* average ability from your class. If you explain the materials to him as he works, you may be able to spot potential trouble areas prior to making the recording. Have the student work through all materials accompanying the tape to make sure they are appropriate.

3. *Type the script for the final tape double-spaced. Leave* a wide margin on the right side so you have room to take notes as the editing proceeds.

CONTENT

Special consideration must be given to several areas:

1. *Watch the vocabulary level.* Be sure to use terms the children will understand. Provide synonyms, explanations, and definitions where appropriate.

2. *Be sure the child is active in some way during or after the tape presentation.* Ask him to respond to the information or sounds he hears by writing a word, solving a problem, or drawing a picture.

3. *Avoid giving complex directions for complex activities.* If the lesson requires the child to listen for a long period before beginning the activity, the activity itself should be relatively simple and enjoyable to perform.

4. *Vary activities at the audio center.* Avoid having the children use it only for drill.

5. *Proceed from the known to the unknown.* Base present tasks on previously developed knowledge and skills.

6. *Teach the students to listen to tapes several times if* repetition is essential to understanding.

7. *Make the tapes as short as possible.* A three-minute tape may be sufficient for some activities, but others may require as much as twenty minutes. Keep the attention span of the children in mind at all times.

VOICE

The way you use your voice is very important. Its volume, tone, and speed all carry meaning for the children. Speak in a conversational tone.

Enunciate clearly.

Use a musical background where appropriate. Music can establish a mood or serve as a transition during a pause.

Use sound effects to enhance stories.[4]

Check to see that distracting speech habits are not recorded.

MECHANICS

It is best to approach the use of audio equipment with a cautious attitude. Read the operations manual that comes with the recorder, and consult a good audiovisual equipment operations manual for special suggestions.[5]

1. Do not vary the distance between your face and the microphone while recording. This movement will change the volume of the finished tape.

[4] John E. Morlan, *Preparation of Inexpensive Teaching Materials* (New York: Intext, Chandler Publishing Co., 1971). This book gives detailed information on basic equipment and explains how to set it up for recording from various sound sources.

[5] Raymond L. Davidson, *Operation of Audiovisual Machines* (New York: International Textbook Company, 1969).

2. If the student must perform time-consuming operations as he listens, prepare the recording so that the student stops the tape periodically while he works.

3. Use a buzzer, a bell, or music to indicate to the student when he should stop the tape. The selected signal should be explained to the student in the recorded introduction to the tape. A musical interlude makes an especially pleasing stop signal.

4. When making drill tapes, pause long enough to allow the student to respond while the tape is running.

5. Give thorough directions for the use of materials and activities accompanying the tape. Some teachers prefer to remind students on the tape to check if they have all the materials at hand. The recorded message then goes on to list what they should have—black paper, green crayon, or ruler, for example.

6. Record your voice just below the distortion level. Make several practice runs to check the volume and other details before making the final recording.

7. Use the tape counter as a reference by writing the counter numbers in the margin of your script every paragraph or so. If you pause slightly between paragraphs, you will have room to make corrections.

COMBINATION AUDIO-VIEWING CENTER

Many learning activities can be greatly enhanced if audio and visual materials are combined in a multimedia approach to instruction. Inexpensive filmstrip viewers and cassette tape players make this arrangement easily within the reach of most school budgets. Teachers may combine purchased filmstrips with teacher or student narrations to develop excellent learning packages. Two students, for example, can use a simple viewer, a cassette recorder, and an inexpensive audio sound distribution system to view and listen to an illustrated story as part of a literature and creative writing lesson.

Concluding Thoughts

The lack of appropriate materials and equipment has often inhibited the development of individualized instruction in the typical American classroom. It was long assumed that expensive equipment was essential to success in individualizing instruction. Creative new ideas and techniques, field tested in many classrooms, have proved that teachers willing to invest both time and effort can provide a rich and stimulating environment. Materials developed by teachers and students for use in their own classroom learning centers are often more suitable than commercial materials for meeting individual needs. And teacher-made projection-viewing materials can be used to facilitate multi-media offerings on the most limited of budgets. They can make a critical difference in the instructional program.

Selected References

Kemp, Jerrold E. *Planning and Producing Audiovisual Materials*, 2nd ed. New York: Intext (Chandler Publishing Company), 1968.

Minor, Edward, and Harvey Fry. *Techniques for Producing Visual Instructional Materials*. New York: McGraw-Hill, 1970.

Morlan, John E. *Preparation of Inexpensive Teaching Materials*, 2nd ed. New York: Intext (Chandler Publishing Company), 1972.

3

Inexpensive Equipment and Learning Carrels

IN THE past, classroom use of audiovisual equipment has been limited by the substantial expense of equipping schools with the necessary projection and audio equipment. But cost is no longer a limiting factor. Chapter 2 presented directions for the construction of inexpensive screens and other equipment that can be assembled by any teacher, or, in many cases, by children working with the teacher. Here we will look at recent commercial developments in the area of inexpensive projection, audio, and other equipment suitable for individual study or small-group work at classroom learning centers.

Projection-Viewing Equipment

For individual study, a simple filmstrip viewer is most useful. The viewer should be rugged, lightweight, compact, and should stay relatively cool during prolonged use. Several such viewers on the market sell for less than $50.00.[1] Guide sheets can be used to replace recorded instructions when children are working individually with filmstrips. These guide sheets may present objective questions for students to answer while viewing the filmstrip, or they may foster inquiry or call for creative responses. Some teachers prefer to use learning contracts in conjunction with individual viewing activities.

A filmstrip viewer suitable for simultaneous use by two children may be even more useful than the individual type. This viewer will necessarily be larger than the previous one, but it should still meet the suggested criteria of size and weight.[2]

If three students need to view a filmstrip at the same time, a viewer with a relatively large screen is required. A fine viewer which will give excellent, dependable service can be purchased for less than $50.00.[3] When using a viewer of this type, be sure to position it so that the back of the projector faces the window. Ambient light falling on the screen will significantly diminish the intensity of the image.

Many learning centers will be designed for use by one to six or seven children working at the same time. Under these conditions, a small, inexpensive filmstrip or slide projector will prove to be the best buy. For about $50.00 you can choose from a variety of lightweight, rugged, and reliable projectors suitable for use with small screens.[4] Children in the primary grades can learn to operate the equipment themselves after only a minimum of instruction, and maintenance is both simple and inexpensive.

A combination viewer-projector[5] which costs less than $50.00 is also a useful tool for individual study and small-group work. Because some parts must be changed when switching from the screen for individual viewing to projection for small groups, some mechanical problems may occur after prolonged use. These problems, however, are relatively simple to rectify.

Motion picture projectors can provide students with the film experiences that are sometimes essential for in-depth understanding. Teachers fortunate enough to have 16mm projectors at their disposal should use them to full

[1]One of the most rugged and dependable viewers on the market is the Viewlex Previewer, Jr., Viewlex, Inc., Holbrook, Long Island, NY. The screen is too small for group work but ideal for individual viewing.

[2] Hudson Photographic Industries, Inc., Irvington-on-Hudson, NY 10533, produces an excellent small viewer, model #331-2. Write to them for their catalogue of projection equipment.

[3]A line of viewers and combination viewer—cassette players is available from Grafex Division, The Singer Company, 3750 Monroe Avenue, Rochester, NY 14603.

[4]The Prima Filmstrip Projector and Prima Slide Projector are excellent machines for the price. They may be purchased from Hudson Photographic Industries (see footnote 2 above).

[5]Sawyer's Projector/Viewer #439-M1, GAF Corporation, Portland, OR, allows for individual viewing on a small, built-in screen, and for projection on a larger screen for small-group work.

advantage whenever films fit into the curriculum. In most instances, however, the school will have only two or three projectors which must be shared by the entire staff. Because 16mm projectors are relatively expensive, it is recommended that inexpensive, silent 8mm cartridge-load projectors be used for small group and individual study at classroom learning centers. Cartridge-load projectors are easy to operate, compact, and portable. Technicolor Corporation[6] has marketed a line of standard 8mm and super 8mm silent projectors costing less than $100.00 which are adequate for classroom use. If you work with inexpensive 8mm silent film loops, you will probably want to provide students with printed guide sheets that tell them what to look for and suggest follow-up activities. Or you can ask students to write individual learning contracts designed to be used with motion picture presentations.

When selecting inexpensive projection equipment, always try it out under conditions similar to those you will experience in your classroom. Be sure that spare parts are easy to obtain and that maintenance service is readily available. Order extra projection lamps when purchasing the equipment. Because inexpensive projectors seldom have fans to blow away the heat created by the projection lamp, some equipment may become

[6]Inexpensive 8mm silent projectors and 8mm sound projectors that use cartridge load loop films are available from Technicolor, Inc., 1300 Frawley Drive, Costa Mesa, CA 92627.

hot after prolonged use. Caution students about this problem as necessary. Be sure that the wiring for power cords is safe and rugged enough to withstand classroom use.

Audio Equipment

Some teachers may have access to record players for listening activities, while others may be assigned a tape recorder. In either case, it is desirable to have an audio distribution system complete with earphones, so individuals or small groups working at the audio center will not disturb the other children.

AUDIO DISTRIBUTION SYSTEMS

The teacher who wants to purchase audio distribution equipment for the classroom can choose from sophisticated built-in systems and simple jack box and patch cord arrangements. For those unable to purchase the more expensive equipment, the least costly approach is to buy an assembled jack box and patch cord from an electrical supply house. Patch cords are used to connect the sound source to the sound distribution system. Jack boxes are simply plugs for earphones. When purchasing patch cords and jack boxes, be sure to select the types and sizes that fit your record player or recorder and the box itself. Check to see that the jacks (plugs) in your box match those of the patch cords and that the headset fit into the receptacles in the box. If you order all of these items separately, you may find when they arrive that they are not compatible—and hence useless unless you purchase adaptors.

Multiple channel phone panel sets allow several students to listen to a single sound source simultaneously.[7] The more expensive systems have separate volume controls that allow each child to adjust the sound to suit himself.[8] Jack boxes for private listening can also be purchased from many electrical supply houses. They can be used with transistor radio earphones the children may bring from home, as well as with cassette tape recorders. Be sure that the plug on the connecting cord fits into the jack on your recorder.

Monophonic earphones (headsets) should be selected with care. Check the wattage output of both your tape recorder and record player. Choose earphones that match the output of both of them, because the volume and quality of sound is adversely affected by equipment that does not match. If possible, try out several types of headsets before you choose one. Headsets should be rugged and well constructed so they will take hard use. Connecting cords with right angle plugs will prevent children from pulling wires loose during listening activities. Generally, the less expensive head sets do not have padded ear cushions like the more expensive models, but they will work just as well.

Inexpensive, dual-purpose cassette tape recorders and playback equipment are now on the market, priced within the reach of most school budgets. It is possible to purchase serviceable and durable equipment for less than $50.00, although dual-purpose recorders are more expensive than machines for playback only. When selecting your equipment, be sure that repair service is available, and that a reasonable warranty is included in the purchase price of the machine. Recorders that are powered both by batteries (for portability) and by line current (AC-DC) are preferable. Check to see that sound is relatively free from distortion during playback. There should be no rattles at normal volume setting. Listen to both music and voice recordings to check fidelity. Inexpensive machines typically do not have footage counters (for easy reference in rewinding) and capstan drive (for smoother, more consistent operation). If these features are critical in your operations, expect to invest more money in a recorder.

Be sure to follow the manufacturer's directions for maintaining your equipment. Check record player needles frequently for signs of wear. Keep tape recorder heads clean by wiping them periodically with a cotton swab dipped in alcohol. To avoid a build-up of particles in your tape recorder, use good quality lubricated tapes. For additional suggestions on the care and use of audio equipment and materials, consult one of the recom-

[7]Newcomb Audio Products Company, Dept. AV-3, 12881 Bradley Ave., Sylmar, CA 91342, produces a line of excellent inexpensive jack boxes.

[8]Switchcraft Inc., 5555 N. Elston Ave., Chicago, IL 60630, also produces excellent jack boxes with adjustable volume controls.

mended equipment operation manuals or educational media texts. No information will be given here on the more expensive tape recording and record playing equipment. If your school budget allows you to purchase better machines, consult the companies referred to in this chapter for information about lines of higher-priced equipment.

Audio card readers are especially useful for teaching children who need work on pronunciation, phrase reading, word attack skills, or any other activities involving the use of both visual and auditory stimuli.[9] Words or graphic materials are printed or drawn on cards attached along one edge to a strip of ¼-inch magnetic audio tape. The master recording is made on one edge of the tape. When the card runs through the machine, the master recording plays back, and the student can record his voice immediately after hearing the master. The card is then run through the machine once more so the student may compare his response with the master recording. Teachers may choose to prepare their own materials on blank cards, or they can purchase pre-printed sets from educational materials companies.

Combination tape player-projectors allow for the simultaneous use of cassette tapes and filmstrips. The price of a manually operated player starts at about $70.00. An audio signal—a bell, a click, or some other cue—indicates when the filmstrip should be advanced.

This machine works well for individual study and small-group viewing.[10]

Small, portable, manually powered teaching machines are another useful item for individual study. One small hand-held machine features continuous-loop drop-in cartridges.[11] The student is presented with a frame (bit of information) followed by questions or choices. He can advance the program cartridge only after making the correct response. Thus he knows when he has selected the correct answer, and which answer is the correct one. Programs are currently available in several subject areas and cost about as much as a filmstrip. Loop production kits are also available, so teachers and students can prepare their own programs to meet specific needs. The machine, complete with a sample program, sells for under $10.00, well within the reach of most instructional budgets. Larger machines designed to handle typewritten or printed sheets of paper are also available, and have proven to be effective in field tests.[12]

No attempt has been made to list all types of equipment appropriate for use in learning centers. The equipment described here is illustrative of what is available to teachers operating on a limited budget.

[9]Electronic Futures, Inc., 57 Dodge Avenue, North Haven, CT 06473, produces an excellent machine, the Audio Flashcard System.

[10]Graflex Division, Singer Corporation, 3750 Monroe Ave., Rochester, NY 14603.
[11]Enrich, Inc., 3437 Alma Street, Palo Alto, CA 94306, produced the machine and program materials.
[12]Grolier Educational Corporation, Min/Max III teaching machine, 845 Third Avenue, New York NY 10022.

Learning Carrels

Designed in a variety of ways, learning carrels can be used to divide study space into smaller units. Pieces of cardboard can be taped together to make partitions and a complete learning center can be set up inside. The unit can be folded up at a moment's notice and stored away or set up in another part of the room. Learning carrels can be designed in a number of shapes and sizes to fit all kinds of spaces.

The accompanying illustrations may give you ideas for designing your own learning carrels. Heavyweight furniture boxes, plywood, and wallboard are all easy to work with. Give them a coat of bright, inexpensive spray paint as a final touch.

The basic assumption behind the use of learning carrels is that students prefer to read and work in a more private environment than is usually provided by flat-topped tables or desks. Most of the following examples (Fig. 3-1-3-5) offer the student visual privacy on three sides, and some can be furnished with individual lamps, bookcases, and jack boxes as well. The carrels are portable—an important feature in any flexible classroom—and they can be adjusted for use by one or two students. As a rule of thumb, study spaces measuring approximately 2' x 3' per pupil are recommended. By reducing distractions and by providing visual privacy, learning carrels can be used to facilitate individualized instruction.

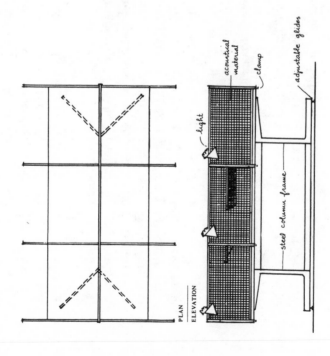

PLAN
ELEVATION

light
acoustical material
clamp
steel column frame
adjustable glides

FIG. 3-1 *Study carrels*
*(courtesy Educational Facilities Laboratories
and The School Library)*

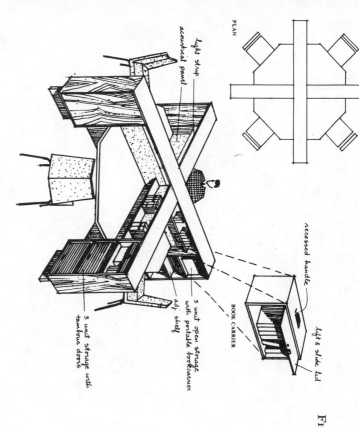

PLAN

recessed handle

lift & slide lid

BOOK CARRIER

light strap
acoustical panel

3 unit open storage
with portable bookcarrier

adj. shelf

3 unit storage with
tambour doors

FIG. 3-2 *Carrels for four students*
(courtesy Educational Facilities Laboratories
and The School Library)

FIG. 3-3 *Carrels for three students*
(courtesy Educational Facilities Laboratories
and The School Library)

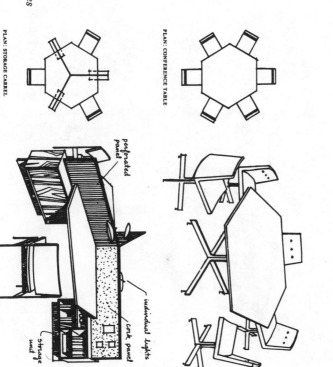

PLAN: CONFERENCE TABLE

PLAN: STORAGE CARREL

perforated panel

individual lights

cork panel

storage unit

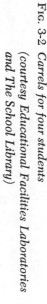

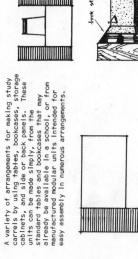
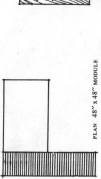
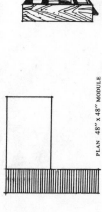

A variety of arrangements for making study carrels by using tables, bookcases, storage cabinets, and side or back panels. These units can be made simply, from the standard tables and bookcases that may already be available in a school, or from manufactured modular units intended for easy assembly in numerous arrangements.

PLAN 48" x 48" MODULE

FIG. 3-5 *Carrels with modular units*
(*courtesy Educational Facilities Laboratories and The School Library*)

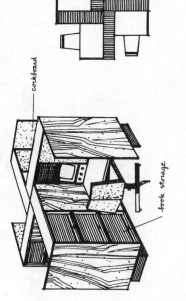

corkboard

book storage

FIG. 3-4 *Hexagon-based carrels*
(*courtesy Educational Facilities Laboratories and The School Library*)

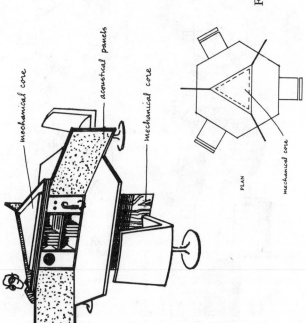

mechanical core

acoustical panels

mechanical core

mechanical core

mechanical core

PLAN

Concluding Thoughts

When purchasing materials and building your own learning carrels, enlist the aid of specialists in your school district. The advice of educational media experts, audiovisual directors, and industrial arts teachers often proves to be invaluable.

Projection-viewing and audio equipment will probably have to be purchased gradually. You may want to begin with an inexpensive filmstrip projector and a cassette recorder, then add other equipment as you can. Arrange your program so that equipment shared with other teachers can be scheduled into your classroom for a week or so at a time, allowing you to arrange for continuity of use over a period of several days. Review the equipment operation skills and train the children carefully so the equipment and machines will not be abused.

Selected References

Davidson, Raymond L. *Operating Audiovisual Machines.* Scranton: International Textbook Company, 1969.

Eboch, Sidney C. *Operating Audiovisual Equipment,* 2nd ed., New York: Intext (Chandler Publishing Company), 1968.

SECTION II

Activities and Materials for Reading Instruction

THE learning center approach is a useful means of individualizing certain aspects of reading instruction. In addition, centers can be helpful in stimulating and expanding reading interests. Content and comprehension, pronunciation and punctuation can all be learned using this approach.

Kinds of Reading Centers

The optimum number and kinds of reading centers will vary from classroom to classroom, depending on student needs. The examples described here indicate the wide variety of centers that can be designed. In every center, strive to maintain a balance between individual and group activity.

Specific skills center. Assign students to centers of this type on the basis of diagnostic tests. Use materials that are graded in difficulty. The basic reader for your grade level, and for the grade levels above and below, makes a good reference for determining the level of skills to be developed in the center. Include a variety of practice materials (preferably self-correcting) and a number of check and mastery tests. Design some of the materials for independent use by small groups of children.

Interest centers. The plural *centers* is used here to indicate that there is more than one kind of interest center. Some centers are designed to stimulate interests and others to follow them up. Listening centers are most useful in stimulating children to read on a variety of subjects. Excerpts from literary works can be presented in an exciting manner on tapes or records. If a printed copy of the spoken material is made available, the student can read along with the recording, or read the entire work later on his own. This center can have a variety of literature selections and can also serve as the means for introducing stories and readings from other subject areas. Include illustrated selections from science, social studies, art, or music along with bibliographies to give further incentive to the child who wants to pursue a topic of special interest.

Comprehension center. Although this center involves reading skills, it has another emphasis as well. The skills center deals mainly with word attack, but the comprehension center stresses understanding. This center assumes increasing importance as the child's cognitive skills develop beyond low-level recall of information. Include exercises in critical reading, problem solving, inferring, summarizing, extrapolating, interpreting, comparing ideas, detecting argumentation devices, and analyzing propaganda techniques.

Centers for reading in the content areas. In order for children to become skillful, well-rounded readers, they must learn the many specialized reading skills which are specific to the various content areas of the curriculum. They must acquire specialized vocabularies, and learn how to read maps, charts, and graphs.

Sample Objectives

In order for learning centers to be effective, it is necessary to formulate objectives for each one. Objectives are statements of desired outcomes presented in terms of children's behavior. Objectives facilitate the job of finding or devising activities for the center and help eliminate pointless activities. As an example of how objectives can be of help, the operation of one center will be described in detail.

The sample center deals with one element of reading readiness. Its objective may be stated in this manner: As a result of working in this learning center, the child will be able to recognize and name the letters of the alphabet with 90 percent accuracy. You will need to: (1) devise a pre-test to determine each child's entering level,

(2) devise a post-test to determine whether or not the child meets the objective (this can be a mastery test at the end of the experiences in the learning center), (3) determine a sequence of experiences to develop letter-learning skills, (4) design a means of recording each child's performance on tests and learning center activities.

You can administer the pre- and post-tests yourself, or ask an aide or older student to help. Simply present the letters of the alphabet in random order to a child and ask him to try to name them. Keep a record of each child's performance.

Fig. 4-1 shows the letters that the individual children named. It is important that the records be as concise as possible. They should be simple and easy to refer to.

In addition to your record, it is useful to have a contract that serves as the child's record of his progress (see Fig. 4-2). Contracts should be made out individually in consultation with each student. The contract serves as the child's ongoing record and guide to learning. It helps foster independence and teaches him to budget his time.

The first column tells the child where he is to work. In this case, he is to go to the same center—1 (blue)—for each reading activity. However, one contract could involve several centers, even centers in different subject areas. Symbols such as numbers, colors, pictures, or shapes may be used instead of names to indicate centers. The symbol that is placed on the contract should also be displayed prominently at the center.

Grade ———   Year ———

Record of Letter Mastery

Date	Name	Letters Named	
9/21	Robin	caps	OX
		lc	oxr
9/21	Craig	caps	OXBTPR
		lc	oxbtpj
9/21	Wendy	caps	XLM
		lc	tefh

FIG. 4-1 *Record of letter mastery*

The second column, _Activities_, indicates what the child is to do at the center. The symbols are self-explanatory. For example, the picture of the pencil indicates to the child that he is to write, draw, or mark in some way. The faces indicate that he is to work with another child or a particular number of children.

The column labeled _Materials_ indicates the envelope or packet the child should work with. (For the convenience of both the child and the teacher, materials are stored in packets.) The color or number on the contract matches the color or number on the packet. Combinations of colors, such as red-green, can also be used to designate packets.

When a child completes an activity, he checks the _Completed_ column. You may wish to check this column yourself when you see that the child has finished an activity. At the bottom of the contract there are places for the date the contract is marked, the date it is to be completed, the child's name (to show that he understands what he is to do) and the teacher's initials (when the contract is completed).

The first space under _Materials_ tells the child that he is to pick up the envelope marked 1 (yellow). In the packet he will find a tape or cassette, which he puts in the player. (He should be taught how to use the player and be thoroughly familiar with its operation before he uses it on his own.) A worksheet is also included. When he turns on the player, the voice on the tape tells him the name of the letter he sees. The recording repeats this

Learning Center	Activities	Materials	Completed
1 (blue)	and	Tape and worksheet (packet) 1 (yellow)	
1 (blue)	and	Tape 2 (blue)	
1 (blue)	and	Tape and paper 3 (red)	
1 (blue)	Friend and referee	Letter Checkers 4 (red-green)	
1 (blue)	Friends	Letter Bingo 5 (red-red)	
1 (blue)	and	Copy letters and words 6 (green-green)	

Contract date _____ Completion date _____
Child's name _____ Teacher's Initials _____

FIG. 4-2 _Learning contract_

procedure for five or six letters, then the taped voice reviews the letter names as the child looks at them again.

The second space tells the child to listen to the tape and repeat the letter names as he looks at the worksheet. Pauses on the tape allow time for the child to respond. The third line tells the child to listen to a tape that names the letters and to write the letters as they are named. If you provide an answer sheet, this activity can also be self-checking. In the fourth space, the child is directed to take the envelope containing a letter-checkers game, find a friend who has a similar contract, and play the game. The picture indicates that the two will need another student to act as referee.

On the fifth line, the child sees that he should find four friends and play a game of letter bingo. Once the students have learned the game, this is an independent activity. In the final space, the child sees that he should pick up a worksheet and copy letters and words for practice in visual-kinesthetic discrimination of letters. He needs a pencil for this activity.

Six activities are included in this contract. The child can do all six, or he can choose only five. This freedom allows the child to exercise judgment in making choices, a valuable learning experience. If an assigned activity is not available when he has time to work on it, the child can choose an alternative from the others listed on his contract.

If the student finds he cannot complete his contract in the designated time, he can renegotiate his contract. At first, some students will have difficulty budgeting their time. One of the reasons for instituting this learning method is to help children learn this skill. They must also learn to take responsibility for their own behavior. Some children are at a loss when the direct adult supervision of the conventional classroom is first removed, but most adjust quickly.

This example illustrates how the various components of a learning center can be developed out of one objective. The list of possible objectives in reading is endless. Teachers' guides for a basic reading series and the many books dealing with methods of teaching reading often prove helpful in defining objectives. Some sample objectives which may serve to guide you in setting up objectives specific to your classroom situation are listed below:

1. Children will be able to hear the differences between the letters *b* and *p* when they are pronounced at the beginning of words.
2. Children will be. able to pronounce unknown words with 100 percent accuracy applying the final silent *e* rule.
3. Children will be able to apply phonics generalizations to the stressed syllable of multi-syllabic words with 80 percent accuracy.
4. Children will be able to outline paragraphs with 80 percent accuracy.
5. Each child will find and read at least three books in an area that is of special interest to him.

6. As a result of listening to part of a book or article, the child will read the rest of it on his own.
7. The child will be able to state the main idea of each paragraph.
8. The child will be able to list items of information and details from a selection containing statements of fact.

These objectives can be adapted, refined, and expanded in order to fit the needs of specific classes. No grade levels are mentioned because the objectives should be designed to meet to the needs of the children in the class, rather than follow a grade level format.

Evaluation and Prescription

The evaluative activities in learning centers must be criterion referenced (designed to meet the attainment of the specific objective rather than standardized norms). Some objectives do not lend themselves readily to objective measurement, so progress must be determined by other means—observation, for example.

In order to measure a child's mastery of the skill of hearing the differences between the sounds *b* and *d* at the beginning of words you might develop a worksheet which looks like Fig. 4-3.

Put the test questions on tape. Say: "Today we are going to listen to the sounds *b* and *d* at the beginning of words. I am going to ask you to listen for the differences when you hear these letters at the beginning

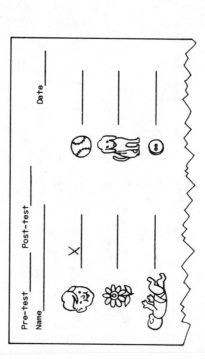

FIG. 4-3 *Worksheet*

of words. You are to mark your worksheet to show you know the differences. Please put your worksheet in front of you and pick up your pencil. I am going to say a word. Listen [Say: *boy*]. *Boy* started with the *b* sound. Find the picture of the boy on your worksheet. Beside the picture of the boy there is a line. If you heard a word that starts with the *b* sound, you are to put a mark on the line. The first one is already marked correctly. Listen once more to the first word [Say: *boy*]. This word starts with the *b* sound, so a mark is put on the line. Trace over the mark. Remember, if a word does *not* start with the *b* sound, do not put a mark on the line. Now I am going to say another word. Find the line beside the daisy. Listen [Say: *daisy*]. This word does not start with the *b* sound, so you do not put a mark on the line. Find the line following the picture of the baby. Listen [Say: *baby*]. If the word *baby* starts with the *b* sound, put a mark on the line beside the baby."

The tape continues in this manner through ten or twelve items. At the end, it instructs the child to turn off the tape recorder and give you his worksheet so that his name and the date can be put on the paper. In the absence of a tape recorder, you can administer the test yourself.

The child's score on this pre-test will determine whether or not he will work in a learning center devoted to identifying beginning sounds in words. The amount of time he spends in the center depends on the child's test performance. Frequent errors probably indicate that a fairly extensive amount of time needs to be spent on that skill.

If you wish to test a child on a greater number of letter sounds, you can include several different letters in one test. In this case, it will be necessary to increase the number of items on the test in order to get an adequate sampling of the child's skill. Similar tests can be developed for ending and for medial sounds.

A simple pre-test for outlining skills is to have the child read several paragraphs of a story from a selected content area. Ask him to find the main idea of each paragraph and a designated number of supporting statements. If he writes or paraphrases 80 percent of the statements correctly, he has met the objective. If not, he should work in the outlining center.

When developing evaluation devices, you should consider these points:

1. The evaluation should grow out of carefully constructed, clearly stated, specific objectives.
2. The test should be long enough to provide an adequate sample, that is, to test the child's actual performance rather than his guessing ability.
3. Test performance determines whether the child goes through many activities, a few, or no activities at the center. There is no point in having a child work on activities in a skills learning center just because it is there.

4. The evaluation must fit what is being taught. There is little point in testing auditory acuity and then assigning the child to a center in which visual discrimination of the letters of the alphabet is being taught.

The assessment of vocabulary acquisition is an integral part of reading in the content areas. In testing children's vocabulary knowledge, it is of little value to have them match words and definitions. It is far better, for example, to have children choose the proper word to complete a sentence from a number of words:

> The wind speed as measured by the _____ was sixty miles an hour.
>
> Choose one word to fill in the blank.
>> hydrometer
>> thermometer
>> anemometer
>> wind vane
>> barometer

Paper-and-pencil tests are inappropriate for reading centers that stimulate interest. Direct observation is the major means of assessment, and anecdotal records are also useful. Questions to ask yourself as you observe the reading behavior of children are: Given the opportunity, do these children read voluntarily? What kinds of books do they read? Do they talk about books? Do they search out books about particular subjects or by particular authors? Do they attempt any follow-up activities, such as writing reports to present to the rest of the class? Do they want to give reports or read selections orally to you or to other children? Do they read at home (can be ascertained indirectly)? Do they have interests which can be expanded through reading? Systematic observations of the children before and after they work in a particular center will reveal how effective the learning center has been in encouraging children both to read and to pursue reading interests.

As in the case of reading skills centers, assessment in comprehension and content reading centers must be based upon the objectives. Some can be measured by paper and pencil and others must be assessed through observation.

Record-keeping Forms

Records, like evaluation devices, must be devised on the basis of the learning center objectives. The main consideration is to keep them brief and simple, to have them easily accessible, and to allow information to be recorded easily.

Fig. 4-1 lists the letters the children recognize. This is a cumulative record which can be expanded as each child learns more letters. Records of this sort can be kept for the whole class on three or four sheets of paper. Other types of records will require one or more pages for each child. Instead of keeping these records in the teacher's desk, it is recommended that the records for each center be kept in that center. Children can go to the center and pick up the appropriate record form when the teacher needs to record assessment records.

Whenever possible, children should keep their own records. The number of words he has learned, phonics elements he has mastered, books he has shared, and books he has read all lend themselves to record keeping by a child. When you write a contract with a child, the child's record forms are a handy reference for deciding what activities to include.

In a reading skills center, a simple checklist makes a useful record. List specific skills on a ditto master and give a copy to each child who is working or being tested on those skills. Two examples of skills checklists are illustrated in Figs. 4-4 and 4-5.

Form A differs markedly from the record form that was presented in Fig. 4-1. That record lists a single skill and the names of all the children in the class, while Form A lists several skills for a single child. The form in Fig. 4-1 has the advantage of greater specificity, but Form A is more convenient. Form B contains both statements of the

FORM A

Name _____	Date _____
Readiness Skills Checklist	

Skill	Mastered
Letter matching (capitals)	
Letter matching (lowercase)	
Recognizes letter names and matches them to symbols when names are presented orally	
Can name letters when written symbols are presented	
Hears likenesses and differences in beginning letter sounds	

FIG. 4-4 *Readiness skills checklist*

FORM B

Base Word and Affix Checklist

Name	Knows the meanings of common affixes	Explains how common affixes change the meanings of root words	Knows meanings of root words of Latin and Greek origin	Determines meanings of unknown words of Latin and Greek origin with affixes
Rita				
Jeff				

FIG. 4-5 *Base word and affix checklist*

skills to be mastered and the names of the students, thus allowing all the pertinent records to be kept on two or three sheets of paper, but it does not allow space for listing specific affixes or root words. These can be written on a separate sheet of paper.

Another useful and convenient type of checklist consists of a list of numbered skills on one page and a list of children's names on another. When a child has mastered a particular skill, the number of that skill is placed in a space following the child's name. This device can be used for punctuation as well as spelling skills.

The wheel record is another type of record which the child can keep himself. It is used as part of an interest center. The child keeps this record in his desk or locker, and when he makes out a contract with the teacher or works in the center, he takes the device with him for reference. He can determine at a glance which topics he has already covered and which ones he has neglected. Figs. 4-6 and 4-7 show how to construct a wheel record.

The larger circle is about 8 inches in diameter and the smaller one measures about 6½ inches. The small spots drawn on the larger wheel mark where the child can color or paste small colored circles when he has read a book in one of the categories. By spinning the inner wheel and exposing the small circles, you and the child can determine how many books he has read in each category. The wheel in Fig. 4-7 shows that the child has read two books in the mystery category.

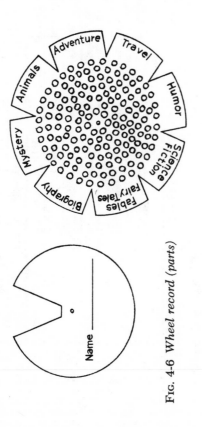

FIG. 4-6 *Wheel record (parts)*

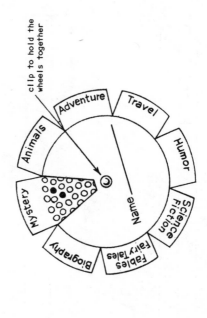

FIG. 4-7 *Wheel record (assembled)*

Self-checking Devices

Excellent resources for reading centers can be made from basic readers in current use, library books, textbooks in various subject areas, old workbooks, discarded basic readers, magazines, and newspapers. You can cut up back copies of books and magazines and include them directly in the center and leave current materials intact. Individual pages from old workbooks can be placed in the center in self-checking devices. Current workbooks can be put directly in the center or in a convenient location elsewhere in the classroom.

Workbook pages and teacher-made materials can be incorporated into reading centers in a self-checking visograph (Fig. 4-8). The visograph can be made with a standard size file folder or two 9″ × 12″ pieces of heavy cardboard. It is a valuable tool for helping children develop comprehension skills, outlining skills, rhyming skills, letter-matching skills, and vocabulary.

The left side of the visograph is an oaktag pocket that holds one to six worksheets with color-coded tabs. The right side is clear acetate. The child inserts the worksheet in the clear acetate pocket, then marks his answers on the acetate using a grease pencil. When he is finished, he removes the worksheet, reverses it, and puts it back into the clear acetate pocket. The answers are written on the back side of the worksheet, and the child matches these against his marks, thus getting immediate feedback on his work.

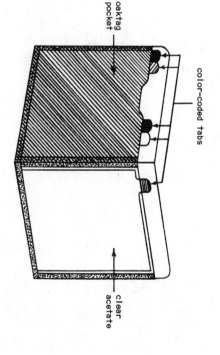

oaktag
pocket

color-coded tabs

clear
acetate

Fig. 4-8 *Self-checking visograph*

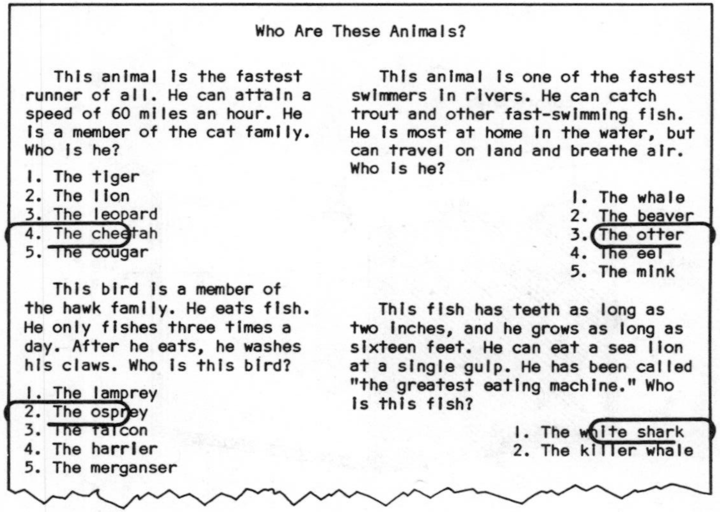
Who Are These Animals?

This animal is the fastest runner of all. He can attain a speed of 60 miles an hour. He is a member of the cat family. Who is he?

1. The tiger
2. The lion
3. The leopard
4. The cheetah
5. The cougar

This bird is a member of the hawk family. He eats fish. He only fishes three times a day. After he eats, he washes his claws. Who is this bird?

1. The lamprey
2. The osprey
3. The falcon
4. The harrier
5. The merganser

This animal is one of the fastest swimmers in rivers. He can catch trout and other fast-swimming fish. He is most at home in the water, but can travel on land and breathe air. Who is he?

1. The whale
2. The beaver
3. The otter
4. The eel
5. The mink

This fish has teeth as long as two inches, and he grows as long as sixteen feet. He can eat a sea lion at a single gulp. He has been called "the greatest eating machine." Who is this fish?

1. The white shark
2. The killer whale

FIG. 4-9 *Clip-check worksheet (front)*

The color coding indicates the particular skill to be practiced, and the skills are listed on the front of the visograph with the color code. The self-checking visograph can be used at any grade level. It is particularly helpful for working on comprehension skills, but it can be used for letter and word matching as well.

Another self-checking device is the clip-check worksheet, used for multiple choice and true-false items. To make this device, type the questions from the left side of the page toward the center and from the center toward the right side of the page. Type the answers directly below the questions, at the far left or the far right, as shown in Fig. 4-9. The child attaches a paper clip over the edge of the page so it covers the correct answer. When he has answered all the questions, he turns the page over and checks the position of the paper clips to determine whether or not he has marked the correct answers (Fig. 4-10).

Tape-recorded Activities

Among the most useful devices in any learning center are the tape recorders. There are two major ways in which they can be used in reading centers; they can help to build auditory acuity and phonics skills and to encourage reading interests. Teachers may wish to include tape-recorded activities as part of all reading centers, or they may develop one or two centers devoted entirely to taped activities.

TAPES FOR BUILDING AUDITORY ACUITY AND PHONICS SKILLS

The contract in Fig. 4-2 lists three activities which involve the use of a tape recorder. The activities described in conjunction with that contract describe how the tape recorder can be used to help children learn letter names.

Self-checking devices, such as folded worksheets, are convenient to use with tapes (see Fig. 4-11).

The tape instructs the child to look at the first line on his worksheet and find the number 1 followed by five letters. He listens to four words, all beginning with the same sound (*fall, found, free, fast*). He circles the letter which he thinks stands for the beginning sound in these words. When he has completed the page, he folds the paper vertically along the dotted line at the right until the two arrow points touch. Now the answers are exposed, and he can correct his own work immediately.

This type of worksheet has many uses at all grade levels. In reading it is used for working with ending sounds, rhymes, medial sounds, phonics elements, and various comprehension skills. This written practice, in conjunction with the tape, helps the child to develop phonics generalizations.

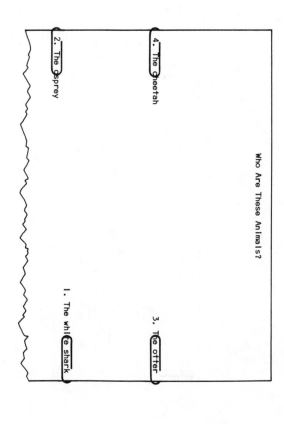

Who Are These Animals?

2. The Osprey

4. The Cheetah

3. The otter

1. The white shark

FIG. 4-10 *Clip-check worksheet (back)*

TAPES FOR BUILDING COMPREHENSION

Children sometimes have difficulty comprehending what they read because of problems with vocabulary. They may be able to pronounce unfamiliar words, but they do not necessarily understand them. This is especially true in the content areas of the curriculum. Use tapes here to present new vocabulary words and introduce concepts before the child reads the selection, and use stories on tape to help the child pick up definitions through context. Teachers' guides for basic readers often contain valuable ideas for introducing new vocabulary, and many of these ideas can be used on tapes.

The child who has a reading difficulty can listen to a story on tape as he follows the text in his book. Later, in class discussions of the story, he will be able to contribute because he has not been penalized by his reading difficulties.

Use tapes also to follow up on the reading of a story, either by presenting additional information or by asking questions for the child to answer. Tapes can also help the students check their work.

TAPES FOR BUILDING INTERESTS

Book reviews, excerpts from stories, recitations, and dramatizations can all be recorded on tape by the teacher or the students. Place the tapes in the appropriate centers by topic. Give the sources of the stories on the tapes, and include additional bibliographical information as necessary.

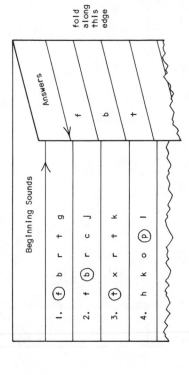

Fig. 4-11 *Fold-and-check worksheet*

Reading Games

Bingo

Popular with children at all grade levels, bingo games can be adapted for practicing a variety of reading skills. The composite bingo card in Fig. 4-12 shows some of the variations which may be played.

Letter bingo can be played several ways, depending on the skills which the children need to practice. First, for letter matching, hold up a card showing one letter and tell the children to cover that letter if it appears on their cards. Second, hold up a capital letter and instruct the children to cover the corresponding lowercase letter. Third, call out a letter name and have the children cover that letter. Fourth, call out a word and tell the children to cover a letter which starts, ends, or is in the middle of that word.

Blend bingo is played in the same way as letter bingo, using blends instead of letters. Play wordo by reading a list of words that children should recognize on sight and ask them to cover the spaces which contain these words.

To make cards for these games, choose twenty-four words and write them in random order in the squares on the first card. Then, using the same words, take the words from the first two spaces and write them in the last two spaces on the second card. The rest of the words then move up two spaces. Change the relative position of the words on each card in this manner, so only one child can

Letter Bingo	Wordo	Phono	Blend Bingo	Synonym Antonym
A a	look	pl	pl	big
R r	yellow	tr	str	short
M	are		bl	fill-in bingo
T	you	br	scr	
b	for	bl	pr	

Fig. 4-12 *Composite card for bingo-type games*

cedure can be followed using comprehension questions instead of words.

Another variation uses initial consonants or blends printed on the chalkboard. When a child lands in a particular square (containing *sh*, for example) he picks up a phonogram card (*ook*, for example). He then reads the word they form: *shook*. He can check to determine whether or not this combination is a word by looking at the back of the phonogram card, where all the words that combine initial letters and blends with *ook* are listed.

Task Cards

Children can expand their reading interests and learn how to go about library research through the use of task cards. Tasks are written on cards and filed in a box categorized by topic or activity.

Read: *Homer Price*
The Mystery of Morgan Castle
Cowboy Sam   (Choose one)

Write a movie script about the story or about one sequence. Pick the people necessary to produce a film (actors, cameramen, etc.). Meet with the teacher to plan the actual filming.

---

get wordo each game. Twelve cards can be made using the same set of words.

Fill-in bingo is a variation of wordo that uses words chosen from specific reading lessons. Give each student a card with blank squares. List the selected words on the chalkboard and instruct the children to copy them into the squares in random order. In synonym or antonym bingo, call out a word and tell the students to mark its synonym or antonym on their cards.

Phono is played in a slightly different manner. In addition to a card containing initial blends, give each child several small cards containing phonograms, *ace* for example. Then call a word such as *place*. The child locates the blend *pl* on his card of initial blends, then finds the blend *ace* on the small card of phonograms and places them together to form the word *place*. Once the students learn these games, they can play them independently in small groups.

Checkers

Children can play checkers in the standard manner, using a board with words printed in every other square. Before he can move a checker, the child must pronounce the word in the chosen square. Variations include giving synonyms or antonyms for words on the board. The game can also be played on a blank checker board. As a child moves, his opponent draws a card and reads the word that is printed on it. The first child must spell the word correctly in order to complete his move. The same pro-

Note that this card allows for a wide range of reading abilities. It also encourages independent decision-making by allowing the child to decide which book to read, which scene to film, and which people he needs to make the film. This is an important element in learning centers.

These are just a few sample games and devices which may be readily incorporated in reading learning centers. The sources at the end of the chapter present many more.

Reading Contracts

Contracts are an integral part of classroom learning centers. Usually, a contract is written to fit the needs of an individual child and should be made out in conference with that child. Therefore, although the contract form can be made ahead of time, the tasks to be performed must be filled in later.

The partial contract in Fig. 4-13 shows two of the five or six activities it includes. The first activity involves the use of a visograph. The child can check off items as he completes them; the teacher can correct his work and check the mastery column for him. The second activity also involves the visograph, and is designed to help the child analyze conversational writing. The rest of the contract is self-explanatory.

Contracts can take a variety of forms and include a variety of activities. Some primary-grade teachers decorate or draw pictures on student contracts in order to

Name _____   Date _____

Center	Activity Number	Activity and Instructions	Materials Needed	Mastery Test or Activity Complete
3 Compre-hension	1	Self-checking Sequential order	Grease pencil	
3 Compre-hension	2	Self-checking Who said it? When?	Grease pencil	

Contract to be completed _____

FIG. 4-13 *Sample contract*

READING SKILLS CONTRACT

Start →

Center*Packet		Check Test	Center*Packet		Check Test	

Center*Packet
1   3
2

Check Test
1

Center*Packet
1   4
2   4

Check Test
2

Confer-
ence with
teacher

Center*Packet
3   3
4

Check Test
3

Center*Packet
3   3
4   4

→ etc.

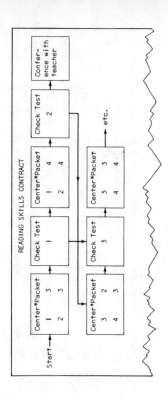

Fig. 4-14 *Illustrated contract*

READING INTEREST OR BOOK-SHARING CONTRACT

Read:

Four Famous Adventures

Adventures under the Sea

Johnny Tremaine

Record or tell the rest of the class one of the adventures in dramatic fashion.

Write a book review of one of the adventures for our school literary magazine.

Record your impressions of the character of Johnny Tremaine before his "accident," after he injured his hand, and at the start of the war. You can write your comments or use the tape recorder.

You are responsible for at least one book and one activity.

Fig. 4-15 *Branching contracts*

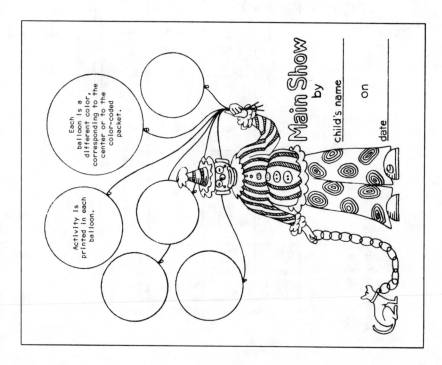

Main Show
by
child's name
on
date

Each balloon is a different color, corresponding to the center or to the color-coded packet.

Activity is printed in each balloon.

maintain a high level of interest. A sample illustration is shown in Fig. 4-14, but it does not include the activities. In the intermediate grades, branching contracts add interest and allow children to choose among several activities and materials. Two branching contracts are illustrated in Fig. 4-15.

The first contract indicates the center and the packet the child must work with. The arrows indicate where he is to go next. After completing the work in centers 1 and 2, the child takes a check test. If he passes it, he can challenge check test 3, or can work in centers 3 and 4 and then take check test 3. If he does not pass check test 1, he must do additional work in centers 1 and 2. He then takes check test 2. If he passes, he can either take check test 3 or go to centers 3 and 4. If he does not pass, he must consult with the teacher.

The second contract tells the child to read *Four Famous Adventures*. He then can choose to do one or both of the activities to which the arrows point. The child also has another option. He may choose to do neither of the activities at this time, but may read *Adventures under the Sea* and then do one or two activities. If he wishes, the child may skip the activities again and go on to read *Johnny Tremaine*. Then he can choose to do any one or two activities, or he may do all three. If he decides to do an activity associated with *Johnny Tremaine*, he must do the third activity, because that is the only one to which the arrow from that book title points. There are a number of options in this contract; the only requirement is that the child read one book and do one activity.

Concluding Thoughts

From these descriptions of kinds of learning centers for reading, a variety of specific behavioral objectives, evaluative techniques, types of records, kinds of contracts, and materials for learning centers can be adapted to set up a learning center program that fits the needs of specific classrooms.

Selected References

Hall, Nancy. *Rescue*. Stevensville, Mich.: Educational Services, 1969.
This book is subtitled "A Handbook of Remedial Reading Techniques for the Classroom Teacher." Included are many useful ideas and techniques which lend themselves to a learning center approach for both remedial and more able readers.

Herr, Selma. *Learning Activities for Reading*, 2nd ed. Dubuque, Iowa: Wm. C. Brown, 1970.
Highly specific activities for strengthening a variety of reading skills, including readiness skills, are presented here. Many reading games and devices are explained, and details of construction are included. One section, made up of a sequence of reading development by categories, can serve as a grade level guide for selecting appropriate activities.

McHugh, Walter, and Walter F. Houss. *The Teachers Reading Program—Newhall Reading Guide*, rev. ed. Hayward, Calif.: JS2, Inc., 1971.
This book is valuable for the number of games and activities it presents that fit the learning center format. Many of the materials can be taken directly from the book. Statements of objectives are included, along with many useful assessments and test ideas.

Russel, David H., and E. E. Karp. *Reading Aids through the Grades*, rev. ed. New York: Teachers College Press, Columbia University, 1951.
Descriptions of many useful ideas, games, and learning devices are presented in this reference.

Stanford, Adrian, and Diane Keech. *Audio Reading Progress Laboratory*. Palo Alto, Calif.: Educational Progress Corp., 1970.
Although not a reference for establishing learning centers, this resource illustrates pre- and post-testing ideas and a coordinated program using tapes and workbooks. These materials can be used to make a fine, complete learning center.

Schubert, Delywn, and Theodore Torgerson. *Improving Reading through Individualized Correction*, 2nd ed. Dubuque, Iowa: Wm. C. Brown, 1968.
This is an excellent reference for materials to use in reading centers. In addition to discussing some probable causes of reading difficulties, it includes dozens of useful games and devices.

Activities and Materials for Mathematics Instruction

5

MATHEMATICS is an area of the curriculum that lends itself readily to learning center instruction. As children approach any new topic in mathematics, they need to experience a great variety of exploratory, concrete, and manipulative activities. As they move from concrete to abstract thinking, they need instruction from the teacher and individual tutoring. At other times, they need lots of drill and practice in order to maintain previously learned skills, particularly in computation. In order to meet all these needs at the same time, you might consider establishing several learning centers for mathematics. Centers that emphasize team learning and self-direction will free the teacher to approach the needs of her students from several sides at once. Regardless of its topic, each center should be arranged to help each child reach specific objectives.

Ideally, the classroom should be organized into a laboratory for learning. Each laboratory center has specific tasks that the children can work on as teams. It is best to begin by repackaging the typical mathematics methods and materials into five or more learning centers. Supply instructions and answer keys at each center along with the materials. The learning center thus becomes a place where children can work together and discuss their tasks. As a team, they find answers to the following questions: What do the directions mean? What is to be done? How should we proceed? How can we help one another to obtain the proper and best results? The tasks may consist of highly specific assignments, a set of options from which the children can choose, or a number of open-ended activities. The teacher decides, as she organizes the centers, which sort of tasks she wants to emphasize.

In designing learning centers for mathematics, consider the following types: interest, textbook topics, drill and practice, programmed materials and devices, measures, application, and problem solving. You may decide to begin with only one center, perhaps an interest center on geometry. Whenever you begin, make sure that the schedule allows time for the children to use the center daily. It is not worth the time and effort it takes to make a center unless specific plans are made for its routine use. The center must be more than a place where children can go after their work is done. Unless it is intrinsic to the mathematics program, the learning center will have little meaning for the children.

The interest center for mathematics should contain a great variety of materials likely to intrigue the children. Consider the following examples:

Time

OBJECTIVE: To learn the meaning of time in various contexts.

MATERIALS: Deposit all kinds of timing devices here—alarm clocks, electric clocks, sand clocks, stop watches, broken clocks, toy clocks, egg timers, candles marked as timers. Gather a pile of printed matter—books, pictures, time-zone information, and timetables for buses, trains, and airplanes. In addition, do not hesitate to use regular textbooks and library or children's books. These can be keyed with colored strips of paper at the appropriate pages. To encourage the children to investigate all these materials, suggest topics for them to study. Write the topics with felt pen on notices for the bulletin board, on large sheets of paper, or on task cards. The questions or tasks are used to stimulate and focus the child's interest and should not restrict his interest or choices.

TASKS:
· How many clocks can you find?
· How does an alarm clock work?
· Can you make a water clock?
· If you were a clock, what would you think of people?
· List the ways you use time each day.

Math Puzzles and Games

OBJECTIVE: To develop specific computation skills.

MATERIALS: All kinds of paper and pencil puzzles and math teasers can be used here, such as follow-the-dots, graphing pictures by coordinates, function rule or number pairs, or computational short cuts such as finger computation for multiplying, halving and dividing to multiply, Napier's rods, lattice multiplication, and similar puzzles (see Selected References for specific information). Games that involve numbers, spinners, or math tasks, such as Quizmo, 3-D tic-tac-toe, equations, Battleship and attribute sort games also add interest to skills practice. Or the children can be allowed to select from a variety of other games and puzzles and follow the directions themselves.

Math in Cars

OBJECTIVE: To provide practice in applying math skills to practical situations.

MATERIALS: Toy cars, motorcycles, and trains, and all kinds of books and pamphlets about cars can be gathered for this activity. Advertising brochures containing pictures and data, newspaper display ads, automobile want ads, owner's manuals, and library books on modes of transportation all make excellent references.

TASKS:

- Find the two cars you like best. Which one is the best buy? Why?
- Which cars are the fastest? Show the speeds of six cars on a graph.
- How fast does a toy train go?
- Write a story about math in cars.
- Prepare a sales talk to sell your favorite car.

Geometry

OBJECTIVE: To understand basic geometric shapes and configurations.

MATERIALS: Geoboards and a set of geoboard tasks; geometric shapes cut from cardboard; solid geometric figures or patterns (nets); pictures with geometric designs, figures, or patterns; and a box of cans, bottles, plastic solids, cereal boxes, and other containers can be deposited at this interest center.

TASKS:

- Try the geoboard tasks.
- How many squares (circles, triangles) can you find?
- List 15 geometric figures in our classroom (in your home, on the playground).
- Build some geometric solids and hang them by yarn from the ceiling of our room.
- Make a geometric collage using circles, triangles, and rectangles.

Math in Nature

OBJECTIVE: To observe mathematical structures that exist in nature.

MATERIALS: Realia such as leaves, branches, pine cones, needle bundles, rocks, cross sections of a tree branch or stump, as well as pictures of trees, shells, and other objects can be used at this center. Nature magazines and science textbooks are also useful.

TASKS:
- Can you count? How many points are there on the leaves, the pine cones, the rocks? How many rings are there on the stump?
- Can you find the patterns? Examine the veins of the leaves, the spiral of the cones, the lines on the shells.
- Can you find the angles? Look at the branches, the leaves, the trees. Draw pictures of all the angles you find.
- Can you find geometric figures? Draw a picture of each one you find and label it.

Inquiry Centers

OBJECTIVE: To stimulate interest in mathematics.

Sometimes a teacher may decide to take the various materials that are deposited in the interest centers and combine them to make a math inquiry center. Any number of the above ideas can be packaged into individual boxes or inquiry packets having one central question. Children can then choose from among an assortment of math tasks that stimulate their particular mathematical interests.

Textbook Topics Centers

OBJECTIVE: To provide individualized assignments.

Because the textbook is usually the most-used resource in the classroom, some teachers may wish to individualize its use. Instead of requiring every child do the same page of the same textbook, the teacher can create basic assignment sheets using similar units from several textbooks. The basic assignment sheet lists all the possible tasks for that topic. By crossing off some assignments and adding others, the teacher can individualize each child's prescription.

The student reports to the station where the textbooks and various duplicated materials are located. He selects the text or pages he needs and either works on them in the center, or returns with them to his seat. After completing his assignment alone or asking for tutoring from the teacher, an aide, or a friend, he returns to the center and corrects his work using a red pencil. The child then takes his work to the teacher for a conference, and together they write a new prescription.

The basic assignment sheets should reflect the standard topics in mathematics textbooks. Rather than blindly following the table of contents, the teacher who uses textbook topic centers is free to reorganize the topics into sequences and tasks that fit her students' needs. The first need is for pacing to accommodate individual learning rates. Second, the teacher can alter the sequence of topics to suit each child. If, for example, one child is confused and frustrated by number computation, the teacher may assign a geometric topic for a change of pace in order to recapture his motivation. Third, if the teacher is using other interest centers, children may report to the teacher station for conferences regarding their assignments.

Drill and Practice Centers

OBJECTIVE: To help the child become more efficient in computation.

The study of mathematics requires a lot of drill and practice. Most teachers recognize the need for periodic, motivated practice after the child has explored and learned a particular procedure. If efficient computing skills are to become habit, then drill is necessary.

Most "new math" programs assumed that repeated exposure to and use of computation on a continuing spiral would allow the child to achieve mastery of number skills. Learning theory disputes this approach. In the near future, children may be able to abandon computing skills as they gain access to machines and simple computers that take care of their need for accurate, rapid answers to arithmetic problems. At present, however, it still appears necessary for the teacher to provide a numbers drill and skills program for each child.

At a drill and practice center, the teacher supplies worksheets, flash cards, and games such as math bingo or Quizmo which are designed to help the child learn the basic combinations. This practice must be motivated, and the easiest way to ensure motivation is to make the task fun. Games that involve several children in a relaxed, informal atmosphere are often the most successful.

Once he is motivated to practice, the child must work on the particular set of facts or computations he needs to master. These may be the easy facts of addition for some children, or the equivalence between certain fractions and percentages for others. The teacher makes this determination. An individual record folder, with a practice and mastery column and perhaps a graph to plot progress, may prove useful. Often it is helpful to have the child time himself on the assigned drill sheet. Three times a week, for example, he can take a time test in the center and record his own progress. When his time and accuracy level reach mastery (as defined by the teacher), he moves on to a new set.

Drill tapes can also be developed for use in audio centers (see Chapter 2). These represent different levels of mastery, such as easy addition, hard addition, easy division, and hard division. For one set of problems, several tapes can be prepared, each with time intervals between problems varying from ten, six, to three seconds. The child begins with the tape that has the longest intervals and progresses to the one with the shortest intervals. A three-second response is a very efficient, immediate recall. Six seconds is adequate for most children. The teacher can also design a recording sheet to accompany each tape. In this manner, the child both hears and sees the problem as he records his answers.

Programmed Materials Center

OBJECTIVE: To provide self-directing materials and activities.

Sometimes schools provide their teachers with programmed mathematics materials, simple teaching machines, or commercial mathematics kits that emphasize developmental number topics. These self-directing materials seem especially appropriate for some children. However, a teacher is often faced with the problem of sharing a few books or self-teaching devices with a group of thirty or more children. By depositing the materials in a learning center, the teacher can give all the children access to the materials on a staggered basis. Each child need only use that part of the material that is appropriate for him.

If only a few programmed books are available, cover the page with a sheet of plastic and let the children mark on it with a grease pencil. This system allows many children to use the same programmed booklet. A commercial drill and practice kit, such as that distributed by Science Research Associates or Singer can become a center in itself (see Selected References).

A single teaching machine is also a self-contained center. Sometimes one or two such teaching aids turn up on dusty shelves in supply rooms, though teachers often fail to use them because there are not enough for the entire class to use at once. In addition, teachers can often obtain from publishers single sample copies of various self-directing materials and booklets. Teaching machines can sometimes be borrowed from the manufacturer on approval or on short-term loan. All these devices make excellent additions to mathematics learning centers.

Measures Center

OBJECTIVE: To investigate the environment in terms of measurement.

The part of the arithmetic curriculum that involves measurement provides the content for many learning experiences. This center becomes not only a place to investigate the environment in terms of measuring length, liquids, weights, time, and other attributes, but it also becomes a place to apply computational skills to problem solving. Measurement centers replace the textbook pages devoted to measures topics and story problems. You may want to rotate topics at the measurement center. Each topic may last for several weeks or a month.

You may deposit assorted materials in this center—realia, printed matter, and texts. Use task cards to direct the student to the activities (see Figs. 5-1–5-5). The cards tell the child what he must do and which materials he will need to complete the tasks. Keep the cards simple in format and use only a minimum number of key words to give directions. Pictures, simple sketches, and references to text illustrations can help give directions and encourage self-direction. For a specific set of task cards designed for middle-grade children showing math as applied in science, social studies, sports and games, occupations, and everyday situations, examine the *Mathematics Applications Kit* (see Selected References).

As a center for liquid measures, the sink area is an excellent place to deposit all kinds of bottles, measuring cups, spoon measures, pints, quarts, gallon containers, and an accompanying set of task cards. One simple task might be to find how many cups are equivalent to a pint, a quart, or a gallon. Another task might entail taking a random set of bottles of various shapes and sizes and

#1 Temperature

Find temperature of:
- hot water
- cold water

Do	Use	Record
	Thermometer	Write: What you did. What you found. Use narrow-lined paper. Name / Date / Task #

FIG. 5-1 *Task card 1*

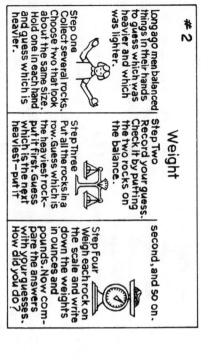

#2 Weight

Long ago men balanced things in their hands to guess which was heavier and which was lighter.

Step One Collect several rocks. Choose two that look about the same size. Hold one in each hand and guess which is heavier.

Step Two Record your guess. Check it by putting the two rocks on the balance.

Step Three Put all the rocks in a row. Guess which is the heaviest rock— put it first. Guess which is the next heaviest—put it second, and so on.

Step Four Weigh each rock on the scale and write down the weights in ounces and pounds. Now compare the answers with your guesses. How did you do?

FIG. 5-2 *Task card 2*

#3 My Weight

Stand on the scale. Record your weight.

FIG. 5-3 *Task card 3*

#4

Draw around your hand

How wide is it? _____
How long is it? _____

FIG. 5-4 *Task card 4*

ordering them from smallest capacity to largest by in-spection. (A sample task card might read: Guess which bottles are smallest, largest. Put them in order of size. Now use cup measures to check your results.) By experimenting and manipulating them, children will learn the units of liquid measure, their equivalent relationships, and how they are used in daily life.

Another measures center might be designed to explore weight. Stock this center with bathroom scales, postal scales, spring scales, scientific balance scales, or even a homemade balance. By using these devices to weigh, compare, order, sort, and quantify all kinds of objects, the children develop an understanding of measures of weight.

Self-instruction Centers

OBJECTIVE: To promote self-direction of learning according to individual needs.

Self-instruction centers can be designed using work-sheets, manipulative devices, and tape recordings. The following example illustrates an introduction to fractional number topics.

Cut pieces of colored flannel (one for each child) into pie-section fractions—wholes, halves, fourths, eighths, thirds, sixths, and fifths. Cut each fraction from a different color of flannel (thirds, for example, might be green). Provide each of the children at the center with a flannel-board.

Develop a tape recording to introduce unit fractions. Then have the children put on earphones and listen to

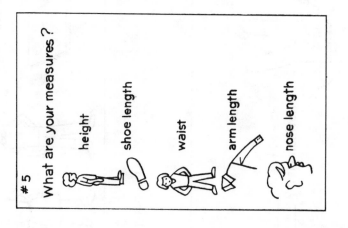

FIG. 5-5 *Task card 5*

the following lesson: "Take out your flannelboard. Put a yellow circle on the flannelboard. This is a whole unit. Find how many red flannel one-half pieces fit on the yellow whole. Turn me off and talk about your results....

Now that you have turned me on, did you find that two halves fit on one yellow whole? Next, see how many orange one-fourths fit on the yellow whole. Turn me off and talk about your findings." The tape continues exploring fractional relationships in this manner until the children can identify equivalent relationships.

Written materials are introduced next. The children write down equivalent fractional relationships on worksheets, then the tape tells them to read the problem: $1 =$ ___ halves, $1 =$ ___ fourths, and so on. They use their flannel shapes to find the answers. Following this procedure, the children can progress through an entire unit on fractions, from exploring and learning fractional equivalents to adding and subtracting fractions with unlike denominators. Of course, the teacher spends a great deal of time preparing the unit. Once it is ready, however, many children move through the self-instruction unit entirely on their own, freeing the teacher to tutor other students.

Mathematics Centers for the Primary Grades

The following descriptions and illustrations explain how one primary teacher arranged a variety of centers in her classroom using her usual teaching materials to facilitate a learning center approach to teaching mathematics. It represents a major effort to involve children in an active, self-directed way in the classroom.

Center 1: Number Topics

In this center you can deposit all kinds of developmental number tasks, beginning with the fundamentals of counting and number recognition and proceeding through the operations of addition, subtraction, multiplication, and division. Include a set of Dienes multi-base blocks with teacher-direction cards.

The Dienes blocks, made of wood or plastic and marked at ½-inch or ¾-inch intervals, represent the unit and positional values of the base-10 Hindu-Arabic numerals. The teacher-direction cards define the ordered tasks through which the child should proceed in order to gain a manipulative understanding of numbers and operations. These tasks begin with the identification of the cardinal number of sets of objects—that is, two blocks have the number property of being two—and proceed through counting, identification of place value, addition of simple numbers, and addition of numbers involving regrouping, subtraction, multiplication, and division. Each phase of these procedures is reduced to a series of steps on the cards. For a commercial program that follows these same steps, examine *Numberblox* (see Selected References).

Dienes blocks can be used in the counting and place-value step, where the child learns to recognize the meaning of a single digit according to its position in the number. In Fig. 5-7, the child is asked to show which is bigger, 12 or 21.

Center 2: Drill Listening Center

Deposit drill tapes, flash cards, drill games, and a commercial drill-and-practice kit in this center. Assign the children to appropriate drill tasks in small teams. Keep individual record folders on file in the center so each child can keep a daily record of his progress. The folders can also be used in individual conferences with the teacher.

Center 3: Task Card Center

Arrange this center at a table near the sink area. A medium-sized cardboard box covered with colorful contact paper can serve as a file box. Deposit about fifty task cards here, all designed to use the environment in measuring and in applying mathematics. Cut each card $8\frac{1}{2}'' \times 11''$ and cover it with plastic (acetate sheets, plastic sleeves, or clear contact shelf paper) for durability. Supply yardsticks, timers, and other measuring devices as necessary.

With a partner, each child takes a card and sets out to find the lengths, weights, liquid measures, time relationships, or money measures it asks for. Then the two of them write stories about what they found. If they wish, students can write headline stories on task cards, then deposit them in a fun box for other children to solve.

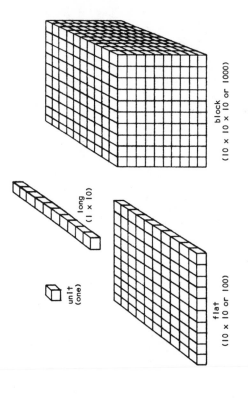

FIG. 5-6 *Dienes blocks*

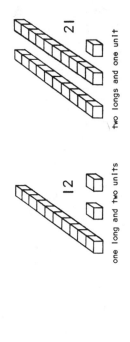

FIG. 5-7 *Counting with Dienes blocks*

The pages of measures and story problems from the math textbook are also made available in this center. The children can use them as challenges, or the teacher can assign them on an individual prescription basis to those children who have completed the concrete explanations and have formed a conceptual understanding of the material.

A headline story written by children might read like this:

We found that Gene is 42 inches tall and Tony is 36 inches tall. We wanted to know how much taller Gene is than Tony.

Do you know? (answer on back)

Center 4: Geometry Center

Deposit geoboards, geoboard task cards, and assorted manipulative materials at this center. Encourage the students to make geometric patterns on the geoboards, find geometric shapes in the room, build solid geometric models, or read books dealing with geometric concepts.

By stitching geometric patterns with yarn, they can explore the lines and curves of geometric figures.

Center 5: Games

Stock this center with all kinds of mathematical games, both homemade and commercial. Ask the children to bring from home any games that involve counting or simple arithmetic operations. Any game that has spinners, dice, or a game board and markers can be used here. Games that have position and spatial distribution (such as checkers, chess, and three-dimensional tic-tac-toe) or coordinates (such as Battleship) should also be included.

SCHEDULING

Each child spends about three days per week at the number topics and drill center areas, and two days at the other centers. During those three days, the child either develops a number idea or spends a small amount of time (ten to fifteen minutes per day) in the drill center. About one-half to one-third of the class can work at these centers at any one time. Assign the remaining students to the games, geometry, or task card centers. You may wish to group the children into five teams according to student needs and organize a weekly schedule to direct them to the appropriate centers. The schedule can either be posted on the chalkboard or written with felt pen on large sheets of butcher paper (Fig. 5-8).

A Geometry Unit for the Middle Grades

In considering the move to learning centers, you may not wish to rearrange the room completely. In this case, you can use a teaching method that is based on activity packets. The teaching of geometry, fractions, and number bases, as well as of the basic developmental number topics, lends itself to this method. First, decide how many subtopics can be made from the main topic, then define each one using a list of objectives and a series of activities designed to meet those objectives. Make each subtopic an individual activity packet. Place the packets in large envelopes or folders and order them in sequence (A, B, C, D, and so on) in a large cardboard box.

Gather all equipment, books, and materials needed to complete the activities in the packets and deposit them in the center. Introduce the children to the center, then allow them to move through the packets at their own rate. Small learning teams can often work together. This style of instruction allows students to go to the center, gather what they need, and then leave to work at their desks or other convenient places in the classroom. Each packet must have sufficient copies of ditto materials, guide sheets, or other material so that each child can have his own copy. Keep resource materials nearby. See Fig. 5-9 for sample record-keeping sheets.

MATERIALS: Textbook unit on geometry, flannelboards, flannel dot lines and arrows, rulers, 1″ × 12″ strips of

Centers	M	T	W	TH	F
Number topics	1	2	3	4	5
Drill	2	3	4	5	1
Geometry	3	4	5	1	2
Measures Task cards	4	5	1	2	3
Games	5	1	2	3	4

FIG. 5-8 *Rotating schedule for math centers. (Each number represents one learning team.)*

tagboard, 4 ice cream sticks of unequal length, cardboard rectangles of varying sizes, paper, tagboard strips, newsprint, colored tissue paper, geoboards, plastic-coated wire in various colors, and empty juice cans.

Introductory Lesson

OBJECTIVE: To interest children in geometry, and to explain the learning packet procedures.

ACTIVITIES: 1. Read the story, "Paul Bunyan and the Conveyor Belt" by William Upson.[1] (Paul cuts a möbius strip conveyor belt lengthwise with his chain saw, doubling its length.)

2. Demonstrate a möbius strip.

3. Discuss the study of geometry and ask children to name geometric shapes around the room.

4. As a class, have the children complete the introductory section of the textbook unit on geometry.

5. Make a record folder for each child and explain the packet system. Staple the record sheets inside the individual folders.

[1]Reprinted in D. A. Johnson and W. H. Glenn, *Topology, the Rubber Sheet Geometry* (New York: McGraw-Hill, 1960), pp. 12-13.

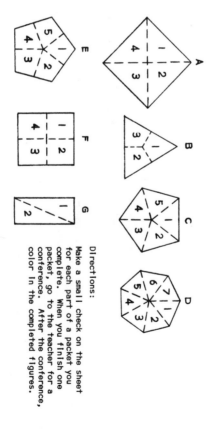

Directions:
Make a small check on the sheet for each part of a packet you complete. When you finish one packet, go to the teacher for a conference. After the conference, color in the completed figures.

FIG. 5-9 *Seven record-keeping sheets for geometry*

Learning Packet A

OBJECTIVE: To define the terms *congruent* and *line segment*.

ACTIVITIES: 1. Complete the appropriate pages of text, then correct them yourself using the teacher's edition.

2. Name the pairs of congruent items in the materials box.

3. Name the congruent parts of your desk and your neighbor's desk.

OBJECTIVE: To use a ruler to measure line segments.

ACTIVITIES: 1. Measure strips of papers from the materials box to the nearest ¼ inch.

2. Complete the appropriate pages of text and correct them yourself.

3. Measure the dimensions of your math text.

4. Measure the dimensions of items labeled A, B, C, and D, in the materials box.

OBJECTIVE: To define and label *curved line, line segment,* and *ray.*

ACTIVITIES: On a large dittoed line drawing of a house and a yard, label the curved lines, line segments, and rays.

OBJECTIVE: To identify curves made from the intersection of line segments.

ACTIVITIES: 1. Use colored pencils and a ruler to connect matching numerals on the following sketch.

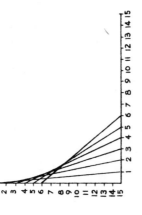

2. Use other basic axis patterns from the packet and build more straight line curves (rectangle, circle, square T, X.)

Learning Packet B

OBJECTIVE: To define the term *plane.*

ACTIVITIES: 1. Stand your textbook on edge. Name all the points that touch the desk. In what plane do they lie?

2. Read the definition of *plane* in the textbook.

3. Name the planes in the classroom. Make as long a list as you can. Post your list on the bulletin board.

OBJECTIVE: To demonstrate the properties of lines and points in a plane.

ACTIVITIES: Take a large sheet of paper. Draw two lines about 8 inches apart. Label the points A and B. Use your ruler to find how many lines you can draw through point A. How many lines can you draw through points A and B? Draw them.

OBJECTIVE: To demonstrate the properties of points on a plane.

ACTIVITIES:

1. Find a piece of cardboard and four sticks of different lengths in the equipment box. Find a partner who is ready for this activity. Working with your partner, hold three sticks straight up on the desk. Set the cardboard on top of the sticks. The cardboard represents part of a plane. How many planes pass through the three points represented by your sticks?

2. Replace one of the sticks with the fourth stick, which should be of a different length. Again, lay the cardboard across them. Does this represent the same plane as in the first activity?

3. Continue this procedure using other sets of three sticks. What can you say about any three points in space and the plane that passes through them?

4. Use your textbook as a reference to check if what you found experimentally is true. (Please return your supplies to the equipment box.)

The remaining packets, C through G, cover other objectives in the geometry unit. The design of the unit involves the student actively in learning geometry experimentally and verifying his results by checking the textbook. Sometimes the activity begins with the textbook, and other times the student is directed to materials or displays to discover for himself what is needed. For example, one activity refers the students to a bulletin board display of buildings at various stages of construction. The child searches the pictures for different geometric shapes and discovers which shapes are structurally most stable. In another activity, the student is directed to build a three-dimensional model. The teacher places an example of each step on the display counter and posts the directions on the bulletin board. The child uses these directions to build the model of his choice.

The activity packet approach pursues the general goal of allowing the child to work through large units of instruction step by step. Internalization of learning is more easily accomplished when daily activities fit into a larger pattern of goals. In attempting to gain this larger objective, the unit draws upon as many different resources as possible to stimulate learning—textbooks and other printed materials, pictures, team discussions, and audiovisual materials. The teacher now becames a resource evaluator.

Concluding Thoughts

In any classroom adapted to the learning center style of instruction, the teacher must have a belief in the child's ability to direct his own learning, to be his own teacher. In a team effort, the teacher and the individual learner are involved in a continuous process of self-diagnosis and decision-making. As he becomes a self-directed individual, the learner enhances his ability to learn and be responsible for his decisions.

In mathematics the ability to explore, to understand, and to use quantitative concepts to interpret the world is the hallmark of mastery. It is this larger goal that should be the aim of all mathematics instruction. A move away from teacher presentations of mathematical con-cepts toward an active involvement in the exploration and discovery of mathematics is most likely to promote success.

Selected References

Arithmetic Fact Kit. Chicago: Science Research Associates, 1969.

Suppes, Patrick, and Max Jerman, *Individualized Mathematics: Drill and Practice.* Syracuse: L. W. Singer, 1969.

Friebel, Allen C., and Carolyn Kay Gingrich, *Mathematics Application Kit.* Chicago: Science Reasearch Associates, 1971.

Lucas, James and Evelyn Neufeld, *Numberblox.* Palo Alto, Calif.: Creative Publications, 1970.

Wirtz, Robert, *Discovery in Elementary School Mathematics.* South San Francisco: Encyclopedia Britannica Press, 1963.

Chamberlain, Jacqueline, "Individualized Geometry Unit." Mimeographed. San Jose, Calif.: San Jose State University.

Activities and Materials for Science Instruction

6

Science is both process and content. Its content is that huge body of knowledge that has been compiled through man's continuous attempts to learn about his environment. The processes of science include all the activities that lead to new knowledge. Because modern educational theory emphasizes the importance of learning how to learn, the modern science program should emphasize the processes of science as well as its content.

Many of the current problems with science learning can be attributed to the fact that science teaching is largely accomplished by reading textbooks rather than actively investigating, observing, classifying, recording, inferring, predicting, hypothesizing, experimenting, and interpreting phenomena at first hand. Learning is facilitated when children are allowed to discover the facts of science for themselves by trial and error.

Classroom learning centers provide an effective means of teaching and learning science in the elementary school.

Some of the key advantages of this approach are:

Science centers can be easily designed to teach science processes.

Less equipment is required if these processes are taught at science centers than if they are taught to the entire class at once.

Science centers can meet the individual needs and interests of each child.

Because less equipment and fewer resource books are needed for each topic, the school can afford to offer students a wider variety of materials.

Science centers enable advanced students to pursue independent research activities.

Once the learning center approach is well established, the children can develop new science centers themselves. Through their research projects, these young scientists can often supplement the teacher's knowledge, thus making the teaching task much easier.

Science Centers for the Primary Grades

The science program in the primary grades should focus on sense perceptions, for it is through his senses that man gathers the information that forms the raw data basic to all knowledge. Learning centers can provide innumerable opportunities for children to use their five senses in identifying and classifying the objects, events, properties, and changes they observe in the world around them.

Science centers should also be designed to help young children develop skills in recording and reporting the information they gather through their sense perceptions. The children should learn how to draw inferences and make predictions about the objects, events, properties, and changes they have observed.

Several science centers suitable for the primary grades are described on the following pages. Both the materials and the processes are listed for each one.

OBSERVATION CENTERS

In science, the term *observation* refers to the use of any or all of the five senses to identify, classify, predict, or infer in terms of objects, events, properties, and changes which occur in the environment. The primary classroom should have a permanent observation center. Because the materials and activities appropriate for an observation center are virtually endless, the center should be changed frequently to provide for continuing growth in perceptual skills.

Touch Box

PROCESSES: Sense perceptions, identification, discrimination, classification, recording and reporting, inference, and prediction.

MATERIALS: Cardboard boxes with fold-down flaps, and a wide variety of objects as suggested by the activities described below.

PROCEDURE: Use as many touch boxes as there is room for in the center. Make some one-hole boxes and some two-hole boxes (see Fig. 6-1). Let the children paint them. Prepare task cards and record sheets whenever appropriate to the specific activity.

The number and variety of activities using touch boxes is limited only by the imagination. The following examples indicate some of the possibilities.

Identification. Place one or more objects in each touch box. Ask the children to identify the object(s) using only their sense of touch. Start with simple objects, such as a pencil, a ball, or a chalkboard eraser. Each time you change the contents, make the game more difficult by choosing objects that are less familiar in the child's environment. There are several ways the child can record and communicate what he has learned from the touch box. He can name the object, answer a multiple-choice question, draw a picture of the object, or describe the object to the class.

Discrimination. Put several objects in a one-hole touch box, and ask the child to find the largest ball, find the cut-out letters that spell *cat*, find the hardest (smoothest, softest, roughest) object, or find the object that has the same shape as an orange. Put several objects in the

FIG. 6-1 *Touch boxes*

two-hole touch box. Ask the child to put one hand in each hole, then find two things that are just alike (one in each hand), find two things that are the same shape but different sizes, or find two soft (pointed, rounded) objects.

Inference. Put several objects in the one-hole touch box. Ask the child to tell what each object is used for. Place several objects in the two-hole touch box and ask the child to find two things that are used for the same purpose. Some possible combinations are: pen and pencil, sponge and washcloth, bottle openers (two styles), apple and banana, and paint brush and paint roller.

Prediction. Line up four one-hole touch boxes. Place some pencils in the first, pencil erasers in the second, chalk in the third, and chalk erasers in the fourth. Ask the child to feel the contents of boxes one, two, and three (in that order) and identify the objects. Then have him predict what will be in the fourth box. Some other combinations for this activity include:

- attribute blocks—large cube, small cube, large sphere small sphere
- one marble, two marbles, three marbles, four marbles
- letter A, letter B, letter C, letter D
- banana peel, banana, orange peel, orange

What's in It?

PROCESS: Sense perceptions, identification, inference, recording, and reporting.

MATERIALS: Assorted boxes (from match boxes to shoe boxes), and assorted objects of various shapes, sizes, weights, and textures.

PROCEDURE: Place one object in each box (a dime in a match box, for example, or a tennis ball in a shoebox). Seal the boxes so the children cannot look inside.

The children may shake the box, smell it, listen to the sound the object makes as it moves, and sense the way in which it moves. They must infer what is in the box without actually seeing or touching the object. There are many variations of this activity:

- From a group of five boxes that all look alike, find the two that have the same contents.
- From a group of boxes, each of which contains more than one object, determine how many objects are in each box.
- From a group of four boxes, find the one that contains an object that is different from the rest.

Other "What's in It?" activities can be designed using bags (see Fig. 6-2). Let the children feel, smell, shake and bounce the bag gently, then try to guess what is in it. They often assume that the round object is an onion. This type of activity can be used to illustrate how our senses can mislead us.

Sounds

PROCESSES: Sense perceptions, identification, inference, recording, and reporting.

MATERIALS: Cassette tape recorder, listening post (optional).

PROCEDURE: Record a variety of sounds which occur in a child's everyday environment—car horns honking, trains chugging, birds singing, water running, doors closing, children playing, cash registers ringing, dogs barking.

The children listen to each sound and try to identify the object(s) involved and the events taking place. They should discuss their inferences with each other. As the children become more skillful, make the task more complex by combining several sounds on one recording.

Children usually respond to all these types of observation activities with a sense of excitement. There is in each of them an air of mystery—something unknown, something yet to be discovered. When we teach children only the content of science through textbooks, films, or demonstrations, we cheat them of the mystery, the search for knowledge, and the sense of discovery which is the essence of science. Learning centers allow children to use the processes of science to discover the content for themselves.

CENTERS FOR CHILD-STRUCTURED SCIENCE

Many teachers feel that they must actively *teach* science concepts to children. Yet, the work of Piaget shows that few elementary school children are ready to deal with the science concepts teachers expect them to learn. This situation limits the child's opportunities to

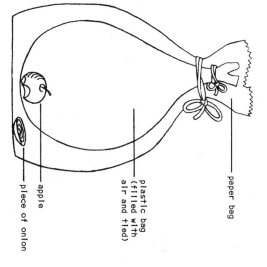

FIG. 6-2 *What's in it?*

paper bag

plastic bag
(filled with
air and tied)

apple

piece of onion

search for knowledge within the framework of his own intellectual development.

Mathews and his colleagues (see Selected References) have recently experimented with a method of teaching science that they call student-constructed learning. Their approach provides the foundation for an elementary science program that presents content, yet is consistent with our best knowledge of how children learn. In this approach, the teacher's primary roles are to:

Provide materials that will capture the students' interest.

Establish an atmosphere of freedom that allows the child to explore these materials in whatever way his own interests and abilities dictate.

Accept the activities of the child as representing his best efforts to deal with the materials.

Ask the child to report on his activities in terms of what he did and what he learned.

Observe the child and make some judgments about his level of development in the scientific skills appropriate for the primary-grade levels.

Because child-structured learning places new demands on the child, he must learn that:

He can do whatever he wants with the materials, within the limits of safety, and with the understanding that he is to keep a record of what he does and what he has learned.

There may not always be a single correct procedure or a single correct answer.

He is free to share his activities and ideas with others, but he should not expect others to tell him what to do.

At first, these roles may be difficult for the child. He has always been told what is right, what is wrong, what to do, and what not to do. The teacher must be patient. Once the child understands his new role in learning science, he will be on his way to experiencing the satisfaction of search and discovery, which is what science is all about.

Blocks and Rods

PROCESSES: Sense perceptions, classification, discrimination, recording, and reporting.

MATERIALS: Cuisinaire rods, Dienes blocks, attribute blocks, other blocks of various sizes, shapes, and colors.

PROCEDURE: Place the materials in boxes at the center. Explain the rules (orally or in writing) concerning safety and general behavior. Give the simple directions: *See what you can learn from these things.*

Because the activities at this center are structured by the child, no list can be presented here. The materials themselves, however, suggest a variety of activities, such as building, categorizing, and comparing. The children should be encouraged to think of new things they might learn from the materials, to try out their ideas, and to report what they did and what they learned. At times the children should work independently, and at other times they should be encouraged to work together in pairs or small groups. In this way, they learn that there are some times when they must rely on their own ingenuity, and other times when it is appropriate to cooperate with others.

Mysterious Magnets

PROCESSES: Sense perceptions, classification, inference, prediction, recording, and reporting.

MATERIALS: Several magnets of differing sizes, shapes, and strengths; miscellaneous objects of metal, wood, cloth, stone, or paper; simple stands, string, tape, small flat boxes or paper plates; and other materials as requested by the children.

PROCEDURE: Place all the materials in the center. Let the children experiment with the magnets. Devise appropriate ways for children to record and report on their activities and what they have learned from them. They might draw pictures of them, tell you about them, report or demonstrate them to the class, or write a story about them.

The materials themselves will motivate the children to explore. The teacher encourages them to try new things, to plan experiments with other children, and to report on what they do and learn. The teacher also observes, provides additional materials, and answers questions.

There are innumerable materials suitable for child-structured learning at the primary level. Some additional suggestions are: live animals and insects; seeds and soil; balance boards with weights, pebbles, or sand; batteries, wire, bulbs; objects that produce and transmit sound (tone bells, rubber-band instruments, rhythm band instruments, nails and boards, tuning forks, tin-can telephones).

The teacher who recognizes the value of a student-structured approach to learning science will be able to think of dozens of additional materials.

FIELD STUDY CENTERS

Study of the content and processes of science should not be confined within the four walls of the elementary school classroom. Science can be taught and learned both inside and outside the classroom. The following activities are designed for use in a field study center.

Shadow Study

PROCESSES: Visual perception, coordination, spatial relationships, predictions, recording, and reporting.

MATERIALS: Box of objects, including washers, puppets, umbrella, lacy valentines, balls, attribute blocks, paper, scissors, leaves, sticks, and so on. Use your imagination. You will also need a clock, a compass, chalk, a flashlight, and a sheet.

PROCEDURE: Place all of the materials in the center. Use a bulletin board or tabletop display to arouse interest in shadows. Write task cards and file them in a box at the center. Post a record sheet in the center so the students can keep track of their progress.

The extensive set of activities presented here illustrates the use of task cards in a learning center. Task cards are especially appropriate for this activity because children can take them outside for reference as they work. The numbers and titles on each card are for filing and recording purposes only. They do not mean that activities must be done in sequence.

---

1. Shadow Study

Take a large leaf to a sunny place.
What kind of a shadow will it make?
Make the shadow lie on the ground.
Make the shadow stand on a wall.
Describe the shadow to a friend.
Draw a picture of the shadow.

---

2. Shadow Study

Join one shadow to another shadow.
How did you do it?
Tell a friend about it.
Make a round shadow.
Make a lacy shadow.
Make a spooky shadow.
Draw pictures of the shadows.

---

3. Shadow Study

Get something from the box to:
Make the thinnest shadow you can.
Make the fattest shadow you can.
Have a friend draw around your shadows.
Draw pictures of your shadows.

4. *Shadow Study*

Make a shadow using something from the box.
Can your friend make a smaller shadow than yours?
Can your friend make a fatter shadow?
Draw a circle, square, or triangle on the ground.
Get something from the box to make a shadow to match your drawing.
Draw something else and try to make a shadow to match it.

5. *Shadow Study*

Put a stick in the ground or use a tree, flagpole, or other tall object that makes a shadow.
Draw around the shadow at 9:00 o'clock.
Draw around the shadow at 10:00 o'clock.
Draw around the shadow at 11:00 o'clock.
Draw around the shadow at 12:00 o'clock.
Draw around the shadow at 1:00 o'clock.
Draw around the shadow at 2:00 o'clock.
Draw around the shadow at 3:00 o'clock.

6. *Shadow Study*

Put a stick in the ground or use a tree, flagpole, or other object that makes a shadow. Draw around the shadow at exactly the same time every Monday for four weeks. Use something that won't rub off.
Draw a picture and write a story to tell what happened.

7. *Shadow Study*

You will need chalk, a clock or watch, a compass, and a partner.
Stand in a sunny spot and face north.
What is the direction of your shadow?
Have your partner draw a line north from your feet.
Have your partner draw the direction of your shadow.
Have your partner draw the length of the shadow.

→

9. Shadow Study

You need a partner.
Can you touch your partner's shadow with the shadow of your hand?
Touch your partner's shadow with the shadow of your foot.
Hide your shadow so your partner can't touch it.

10. Shadow Study

Use a pair of scissors.
Can you make a shadow on your hand that looks like a pair of eyeglasses?
Make other shadows on your hand with the scissors, with other objects from the box.
On paper, draw pictures of the shadows you made.
Show your pictures to a friend and see if he can tell what you used to make each shadow.

7. (Continued)

Write down the time of day.
Repeat the activity exchanging jobs with your partner.
Mark on the ground to show where you think your shadows will be in one hour.
In one hour, check to see if you were right.

8. Shadow Study

You need a partner.
Play shadow tag.
Ask your partner to try to touch your shadow with his foot.
Move fast.
Don't let him catch your shadow.
Get several people to play.

11. Shadow Study

Stand with your shadow in front of you.

Stamp on your shadow's head.

Don't touch your shadow at all!

Put your shadow's hand on top of your shadow's head.

Make your shadow as short as you can.

Make it as tall as you can.

Clap your shadow's hands, but not your own.

12. Shadow Study

Shake a friend's hand in the sun.

What does the shadow look like?

Can you make the shadow of your hand shake the shadow of a friend's hand?

How far apart can you stand and still touch shadow hands?

How far apart can you have your hands and still have your hand shadows touch?

13. Shadow Study

In the classroom make a shadow screen with a sheet and a projector.

Have a shadow boxing match with a friend for the class.

Have the class tell you how the shadows acted.

Join the audience and watch others have a boxing match.

14. Shadow Study

Mark an X on the ground with chalk.

Can you touch the X with the shadow of your finger?

How far away can you stand and still touch it?

Can you guess where to stand to touch any mark on the ground with the shadow of your finger?

Prove it.

15. Shadow Study

Write about all of the things you learned in the shadow study.

Draw a picture of the thing that was most fun to do.

Can you think of other interesting things to do with shadow?

CENTERS FOR CONTENT-BASED SCIENCE

Up to this point, the process approach to science teaching has been emphasized. Learning centers are also highly effective for teaching science activities which focus on the development of science facts, the content-based program, as the following example illustrates.

Sea Life is a content-based science center that breaks away from textbook and teacher-dominated lessons. Through the use of student contracts, the teacher can provide for the individual learning style and rate of each child.

Sea Life[1]

PROCESSES: Individualized learning, sense perception, creative activities, recording, and reporting.

MATERIALS: Filmstrip and viewer or projector, tape, tape player, dittos, paper, pencils, crayons, chart of a fish, magnetic fishing game, language master, typewriter, aquarium and fish, construction paper, scissors, paste, film loop on whales, film loop projector, and sea books.

PROCEDURE: Make all of the above items available to the children. They do not all have to be located at the center. Place the contracts and dittos in a folder at the center. Use a chart, bulletin board, or live fish to arouse student interest. Prepare a record folder for each child.

The activities for the center are described on the contracts. The use of standard symbols makes it easy for the children to understand what they are to do, so they are not penalized for poor reading skills. One complete contract, in four parts, is presented here (Fig. 6-3). In the lower right corner of each contract page is a place for the teacher to check the child's progress.

Science Centers for the Intermediate Grades

Children in the intermediate grades are ready for the higher-order skills of controlling variables, experimenting, recording and interpreting data, and making higher-

[1] This learning center was developed by Debbie Smith, a primary teacher in Santa Clara, California.

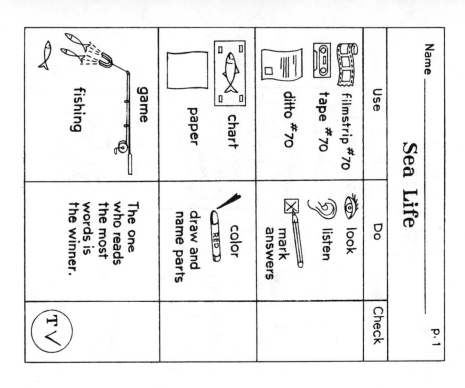

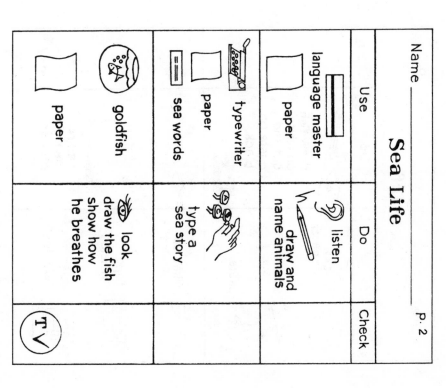

FIG. 6-3 *Sample contract*

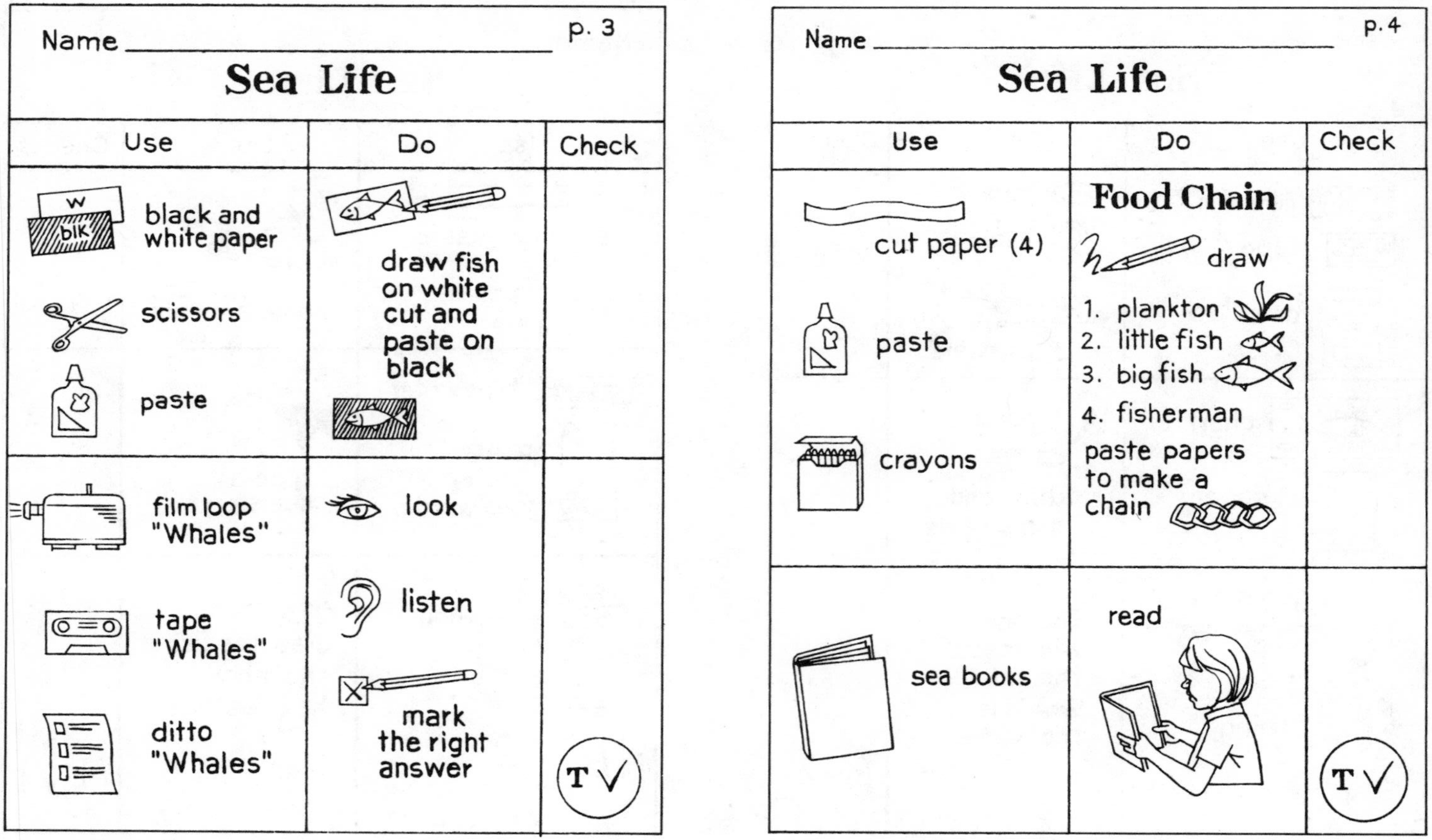

Name _____ **Sea Life** p. 3

Use	Do	Check
black and white paper scissors paste	draw fish on white cut and paste on black	
film loop "Whales" tape "Whales" ditto "Whales"	look listen mark the right answer	TV

Name _____ **Sea Life** p. 4

Use	Do	Check
cut paper (4) paste crayons	**Food Chain** — draw 1. plankton 2. little fish 3. big fish 4. fisherman paste papers to make a chain	
sea books	read	TV

FIG. 6-3 *Sample contract (Continued)*

level inferences and predictions. The activities they tackle must be correspondingly sophisticated. Structurally, however, these centers are similar to those for the primary grades.

EXPERIMENTATION CENTERS

This type of center replaces the observation center used at the primary level. Many of the perceptual skills initiated in the primary observation centers will be further developed in the experimentation center.

Mealworms

PROCESSES: Sense perceptions, experimentation, controlling variables, recording and reporting, interpreting data, creative activities.

MATERIALS: Mealworms, bran and other foods, shoe boxes, cardboard, construction paper, glue, dittoed record sheets, tape, book, matchboxes or other small containers, record player, and pint jars.

PROCEDURE: Place all of the materials except perishable items in appropriate containers. File the task cards in order. Prepare simple record sheets or let the children design their own record sheets for each experiment (see Selected References).

---

1. Mealworms

Place a mealworm on a desk and observe him for a few minutes.

Write down all the things he did.

Compare what you observed with what others in your group observed.

---

2. Mealworms

Select a mealworm for your experiments.

Watch him walk for ten minutes.

Keep a record of how many times he turns to the right, to the left.

Can you make him go in a straight line? How?

Keep your mealworm in a small container with your name on it.

You will want to compare his behavior with that of the other mealworms.

5. *Mealworms*

Place your mealworm on a book. Hold it at a 10-degree slant.

Does he walk up or down?

Try it five times. Record the number of times he walks up and the number of times he walks down. Repeat this experiment holding the book at 20 degrees, 45 degrees, 75 degrees.

6. *Mealworms*

Place a mealworm in a small container with exactly ten flakes of bran.

Place another in a small container with ten tiny bits of bread, another with ten bits of rice cereal, another with ten bits of sawdust. (You also might try dry dog food, carrot, potato, or onion.) Label each container.

↑

3. *Mealworms*

How far can your mealworm move in one minute?

Try this five times and find the average distance he moves in one minute.

Compare your results with those of your classmates.

4. *Mealworms*

Put 1 inch of bran in a pint jar.

Place your mealworm on the bran and hold up the jar so you can look up at the bottom.

How long does it take your mealworm to dig to the bottom?

Try it again.

Record your results.

6. (Continued)

Each day check to see if the mealworms have eaten. Keep a record of your results. What can you say about food for mealworms?

---

7. *Mealworms*

Make a wall using a strip of cardboard.

Put a mealworm next to the wall.

What does he do when he walks to the end of the wall?

Try it with other mealworms.

Do they all behave the same way?

What did you learn from this experiment?

Discuss it with some friends.

---

8. *Mealworms*

Use strips of cardboard to make a maze in the lid of a shoe box.

Place a dozen mealworms in the center of the maze and see what happens.

Draw a picture to show where the mealworms are after five minutes.

---

9. *Mealworms*

Place a small pile of bran near one end of a shoe box.

Mark a starting point about six inches from the bran.

Place a mealworm at the start.

As he moves, draw the path he takes until he reaches the bran.

How long does he take?

Try this experiment five more times with the same mealworm.

10. *Mealworms*

Do mealworms go toward walls?

Cut six 1-inch walls from cardboard. Fold them so they will stand up.

Draw a circle 12 inches in circumference.

Place the walls around the circle so that there are 1-inch spaces between them. This makes exactly six inches of spaces.

↑

10. (*Continued*)

Place a mealworm in the center. If he walks to a wall, mark where he touches it. If he walks through a space, mark where he goes through.

Repeat this activity fifty times and record the results.

11. *Mealworms*

Do mealworms have a favorite color?

Cut out 2-inch squares of red, yellow, black, and blue construction paper. Paste them on a sheet of white paper and cut off the excess white.

Cut a small round circle of white paper and paste it where the four corners meet.

↑

11. (*Continued*)

Place ten mealworms—one at a time—in the center of the white circle.

Record the color each one goes to.

Try it again.

In addition to this biological study of mealworms, there are many physical science topics which lend themselves to experimentation—magnets, static electricity, current electricity, and simple machines.

CENTERS FOR CHILD-STRUCTURED LEARNING

This type of science center was described in detail in the section for the primary level. The following topics are appropriate for the intermediate grades.

Lenses

PROCESSES: Sense perceptions, experimentation, research, recording, reporting, and controlling variables.

MATERIALS: An assortment of concave and convex lenses, cardboard tubes from the rolls of toilet tissue or aluminum foil, long and short modeling knives or single-edge razor blades, masking tape, reference books (science books, encyclopedias), scraps of wood (assorted small blocks), glue, and other materials as requested by students.

PROCEDURE: Place all these materials in a learning center. Instructions should relate only to safety precautions and suggestions such as: *learn as much as you can from these materials or make something.* The only requirement is that the children keep records of what they do, demonstrate what they make, and report in an appropriate way the things they learn.

Following the same procedures as for Lenses, the teacher might deposit the following assortments of items in child-structured centers:

Batteries, bulbs, wire, pliers, blocks of wood, strips of metal (cut from cans), nails, string, and reference books. Let the students experiment, make something, and give reports.

Microscope, slides, pond water, cotton, onion, potato, carrots, celery, leaves, yeast, and reference books. Let the students explore, draw pictures, and report.

Grab Bag

PROCESSES: Sense perceptions, experimentation, research, recording, and reporting.

MATERIALS: Several shoe boxes or paper bags containing a variety of materials such as the following: rocks and minerals, hand lenses; assorted seeds, soil; thread spools, string, weights, pulleys, nails, scraps of wood; caterpillars, plastic wrap, milk cartons, leaves; magnets, scraps of metal and nonmetal objects, iron filings, compass, needles; corks, glass jars.

PROCEDURE: Deposit eight or ten shoe boxes or paper bags in the center. Put one set of materials in each and seal them. Put all the boxes or bags in a large box. Divide the class into groups of three or four students, and let each group grab a bag from the box.

Give children three weeks to learn as much as they can using their materials and any other materials they might want to add. At the end of the allotted time, each group reports its findings to the rest of the class. Awards are given for the best reports, based on knowledge gained, originality of experimentation, quality of the presentation, and other appropriate factors. Be sure that the points to be judged and the method of judging are made clear to the students before they begin to work.

FIELD STUDY CENTERS

Many teachers think that in order to study science outdoors, it is necessary to plan an extensive trip to a forest, seashore, or park. Although these are certainly exciting and worthwhile places to visit, much outdoor science learning can take place right on the school grounds.

A Tree

PROCESSES: Sense perceptions, measurement, controlling variables, recording, reporting, and comparisons.

MATERIALS: Rulers, tape measures, protractor, nylon cord, string, permanent marking pens or oil paint, plastic tags, and data sheets.

PROCEDURE: No special table is necessary for this center because most of the activities will take place outdoors. The materials can be stored in a box or can be brought together just at the times they are needed. Task cards, data sheets, and record sheets can be stored in files.

The activities for this center extend over most of the school year. The first task is to select a small tree on or near the school yard and gain permission to use it as an outdoor study center. If they are conducted properly, the activities will not damage the tree. The project should begin as soon as the tree loses its leaves.

1. Starting at the bottom, number each of the main branches on the tree. Tie a numbered plastic tag on each branch.

2. Measure and record the distance from the ground to the first branch.

3. Measure and record the distances between each of the other main branches.

4. Measure and record the height of the tree.

5. Using white paint, make small marks on the trunk 1 foot from the ground, 2 feet, 3 feet, and so on until you reach the top of the tree.

6. Measure and record the diameter of the trunk at ground level and at each mark.

7. Select three main branches at random. Mark each one with paint spots at 6-inch intervals, starting 6 inches from where the branch connects to the trunk.

8. Measure and record the diameter of each of these branches at each mark.

9. Measure and record the length of the selected main branches.

10. Count and record the number of secondary branches and twigs on each of the three main branches.

11. Use a protractor to measure the angle at which each main branch comes off of the trunk. Record these data.

12. Use the protractor to measure the angle at which the secondary branches come off of the selected main branches. Record these data.

13. Select one main branch. Look closely to see if you can determine where new leaves will appear. Mark these spots with small drops of paint.

14. Predict the number of new leaves that will be on the branch in the spring. Record your prediction. Write a short paragraph to explain why you think your prediction is correct.

15. Record the dates on which each of these activities is completed.

16. Repeat all of the above measurements every two months until near the end of the school year.

17. As the leaves begin to appear, check to see if they are growing where you predicted.

18. When the leaves are fully developed, count how many appeared on the selected branches. Was your prediction correct? If you were wrong, try to determine what factors you did not take into account in your predictions. Could you make a better prediction if you were to repeat these activities next year?

19. Make graphs to summarize your measurement data.

Analyze all of the measurement data you have recorded about the tree. Write a report explaining what happened to your tree. Tell others about your discoveries.

There are many other outdoor science activities which can be conducted on or near the school grounds. Here are two additional suggestions.

What's in a Vacant Lot?

1. With four or five friends, mark off an area 1 foot square on a corner of the school grounds or in a nearby vacant lot.

2. Using small tools, carefully remove each plant, rock, pebble, insect, or worm down to a depth of six inches.

3. Keep records of the different kinds of plants and animals you find and the total numbers of each.

4. Collect and count all the rocks and pebbles.

5. Display what you have collected and write a report about the number of plants, animals, and rocks you found in one square foot of earth.

A Nature Trail

1. Learn the names of the trees and shrubs on the school yard.

2. Are they native or domestic plants?

3. What are their scientific names?

4. What other plants are they related to?

conclusions. We must be willing to allow children to make these same kinds of mistakes.

Selected References

Piaget, Jean, and Barkel Inhelder. *The Growth of Logical Thinking*. Translated by Anne Parsons and Stanley Milgram. New York: Basic Books, 1958.

Mathews, Charles, Darrell Phillips, and Ronald Good. *Teachers Guide: Student Structured Learning in Science*. Dubuque, Iowa: Wm. C. Brown, 1971.

Elementary Science Study. *Light and Shadow*. New York: Webster Division, McGraw-Hill Book Company, 1968.

Elementary Science Study. *Behavior of Mealworms*. New York: Webster Division, McGraw-Hill, 1966.

5. When sufficient information has been gathered, make small signs to place by each shrub to create a nature trail other classes can use.

Concluding Thoughts

This chapter has described only a few of the thousands of ideas that are appropriate for science centers in the elementary school. You need not be a scientist yourself to have an effective science program. You must, however, be willing to provide the materials and then to allow children to use those materials to search for answers within the limits of their abilities and imaginations. You must also be willing to let them make mistakes. No scientist who has added to the fund of knowledge was always right. Each one made human errors and reached false

Activities and Materials for Language Arts Instruction

THE language arts encompass communication skills in listening, speaking, and writing. The wide range of skills necessary to gain proficiency in the language arts makes this an area which lends itself well to the learning center format. Often teachers who are just starting to use this approach begin with some aspect of the language arts. Among the most versatile devices that can be used in language arts centers are tape recordings. Although they can serve a variety of purposes, tapes are particularly useful in listening centers.

Listening Centers

Listening centers can be used for both skills development and appreciation and enjoyment activities. Some centers fit into either category, depending on the purposes for which they were set up. For example, at one type of listening center children can listen to various types of literature—fiction, nonfiction, and poetry. They may do activities in conjunction with the center, or they may listen solely for enjoyment. In either case, they can follow along in their books as the poem or story is read on tape.

At the language arts center, you can direct the students to listen for certain elements of style, such as the effective use of action words. Or you can ask them to interpret a poem. "The Hairy Dog" (from *Pillicock Hill*[1] by Herbert Asquith), for example, can serve as the basis of a number of exercises. At the primary level, a child could first draw his conception of this dog, then describe his own puppy or a make-believe canine in prose or poetry, and record his description on tape. In this manner, the student sharpens his skills of description, and you can easily check his progress.

At a higher grade level, you can introduce students to a variety of writing styles on tape by combing several children's books for some of the innumerable ways that are used to express a simple idea, such as locomotion. *The boy walked*, for example, can be expressed in such diverse ways as *the urchin ambled* or *he loped along*. The students listen to a number of these examples on tape, then compose their own and incorporate them into stories. This technique can be used to introduce a wide variety of stylistic devices.

Pre- and post-tests can also be used in conjunction

[1]Huber, Miriam, *Story & Verse for Children* (New York: The Macmillan Co., 1965).

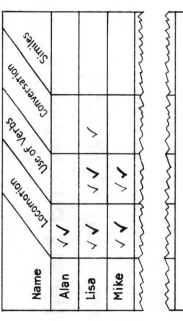

FIG. 7-1 *Record-keeping sheet*

with these tape-recorded activities. As a means of pre-assessment, read a child's writing looking specifically at his style. If the child uses a number of dull and insipid words and phrases, assign him to a listening center that stresses the variety of ways in which basic ideas can be expressed. As check and mastery tests, read the child's later writings and compare them to his earlier ones. A checklist of items to look for comes in handy here. This list can also serve as a record of progress.

The four headings at the top of the form in Fig. 7-1 indicate the four topics that are covered in this listening center. Locomotion, the first one, has already been explained. The second column, use of verbs, indicates that the child needs to develop skill in expressing action using a variety of verbs. The third heading refers to the *he said* and *she said* approach to writing dialogue. The objective here is to help students write more precise and descriptive dialogue such as *he shouted* or *she spoke in a soft whisper.* The objective for the fourth column might be: the child will incorporate similes in his writing where appropriate. At the listening center, deposit examples of similes culled from a variety of literary selections. After listening to the tape, the child attempts to draw a general definition of *simile* and then tries writing his own.

When a child thinks he has mastered a particular writing skill, he checks the appropriate space on the record sheet that is posted in that center. When that child writes his next assignment, you can consult the record form to see which skill he thinks he has mastered. Examine the child's paper in order to determine whether he indeed shows mastery of that skill in his writing. If you agree, place a blue check next to the child's mark, indicating that he may proceed to another center or another skill. If you decide that the child needs more practice, simply erase his mark. The student then reports to you for a conference.

At the conference, go over the paper with the student showing him where his writing can be improved. The child returns to the center, listens to more tapes and works on additional exercises until he masters the skill. Make several different tapes for each skill so a child who needs extensive practice will not have to repeat the same exercises again and again.

Many students find it difficult to follow oral directions. Listening centers are useful in teaching this skill at any grade level; it is simply a matter of complexity of directions. Prepare several tapes for each grade level ranging, for example, from simple directions on how to play easy games, to complex directions on how to fold paper animals using origami techniques. For beginners, give directions one step at a time at intervals of several seconds so they can complete one step before listening to the next. More advanced tapes can include clusters of two- and three-step directions given at once. After the students master the technique, tapes can be used routinely to give directions for language arts activities. In this sense, the tape recording serves as a second teacher, giving directions and explaining activities to one group of students while the teacher works elsewhere.

Other skills areas that can be developed at the listening center include listening to a story for answers to specific questions of fact, answering broad questions requiring generalizations about the story or the characters, or answering thought questions that require inferences about some aspect of the story. Auditory acuity exercises, such as listening for beginning or ending sounds and rhyming elements, can also be presented on tape.

As a motivational device, stories incorporating sound effects can be recorded and kept in the listening centers. The students listening to these stories can enjoy the sound effects as they follow along in the book. Tapes can be used to introduce stories or to complete stories. Tapes made by the teacher or by professional actors will often pique student interest in a broad variety of materials. The works of Shakespeare, for example, can be introduced using recordings made by well-known Shakespearian actors.

Oral Language Centers

If it is generally agreed that oral language is the basis upon which the skills of written language are built, then particular attention must be paid to oral language training. The child must learn to describe his world with precision, clarity, and a certain felicity of expression. Task cards can be of great help here.

Task Card 1

Choose an object or picture from the box at the learning center and describe it to four people in your class. Do not let them see it. Describe its physical characteristics, not its function. Either have them tell you what they think it is, or have them draw it. Try to give the description in as few words as possible. Use 25 words or less, or ten sentences or less.

Task Card 2

Tell a friend how to make a paper airplane (or cut out a snowflake or make a mobile). You may give each direction only once.

These task cards illustrate only two of the myriads of activities that can be used in oral language centers. For Task Card 1, a number of objects (usual and unusual) and assorted pictures (landscapes and action) are deposited in the corner. In order to refine his descriptive skills, the child should be restricted to using a given number of words or sentences. These limits force the student to select his words carefully. In order to eliminate unrealistic restrictions it is helpful to try each task yourself before assigning it to the children.

Task Card 2 directs the children to give oral directions of some sort for making something, trying a particular art technique, completing a workbook page, or playing a game. A time limit can be indicated on the task card. With slight changes, both these task cards can be adapted for use in a writing center.

Other activities which can be written on task cards or listed as contract items include: dictating a story to another child (usually a young child dictates to a child from an upper grade) or into a tape recorder; dramatizing a story (either one that has just been introduced, or an original); trying out various styles of writing (essay, narrative, fantasy, exposition); telling a story in the first person and then in the third person; or trying out various poetry patterns (haiku, cinquain, diamonte, or ballad).

Writing Centers

Skills development and skills application can both be taught at writing centers. In general, skills development involves learning and practicing the skills basic to effec-tive communication—spelling, punctuation, grammar, and vocabulary. Skills application centers enable the child to apply his newly learned skills to a number of writing activities. Check tests and mastery tests must be included in the development centers, but the children's writing itself serves as a check on application.

Among the many writing skills centers, spelling centers are one of the most common. One important source of spelling words is the children's own work. Early in the school year you can analyze the children's writings looking for words they commonly misspell. Another source is the state-adopted speller; this is a particularly useful source of words that can be used to illustrate basic spelling generalizations.

Here, as in so many other centers, a tape recorder comes in handy. Short lists of words are recorded on tape, and the child simply listens to the tape and writes the words. If a master list of words is provided with each taped lesson, the child can correct his own work. You can make the tapes as you proofread the children's stories, dictating the misspelled words directly onto tape. Tapes can also be used for writing entire stories. A story that includes selected spelling words is put on tape for the children to transcribe. Again, each child corrects his own work by comparing it to a master list. Story tapes can be used in conjunction with oral language centers in which a child is asked to compose and then tape stories that include a designated list of spelling words. Recorded stories are placed in a spelling center, where they can be transcribed by other children who need to learn how to spell those particular words.

Periodically, remember to include words from earlier tapes for the purpose of testing. Go over each child's work with him in a conference, then decide whether he has achieved mastery or whether he should continue to practice that list.

In the intermediate grades, writing centers can be devoted to the study of root words and affixes. Present root words in sentences in order to illustrate their meaning. (*Example:* He knew it was possible to walk a mile.) Ask the child to add the prefix *im* to the root word, thereby changing its meaning. After he has written a number of sentences in this manner, ask him to indicate the meaning of *im*. In this way, students can enlarge their vocabularies, learn affixes and root words, and develop generalizations about spelling them.

Spelling Skills Centers

Games such as Scrabble and Spill 'n' Spell provide an enjoyable form of spelling practice. Any game in which the child must move a marker from a starting point to a designated goal can be used in spelling centers. First, the child rolls a die or spins a spinner, then moves the designated number of spaces. Next, he draws a card from a pile of spelling words in the center of the board. His opponent or a referee reads the word, and the child attempts to spell it. If he spells it correctly, he moves forward again as many spaces as he moved originally, but if he makes a mistake, he moves back that number of spaces.

The game board (Fig. 7-2) can be modified in a number of ways for use in both reading and spelling centers. One version of a spelling game requires four sets of cards, each set of a different color. The red cards contain simple spelling words, the green, difficult words, the blue average words, and the brown (shortcut cards) contain words of great difficulty. Provide a spinner with alternating red, blue, and green areas and let the players take turns spinning it. If the pointer lands on red, an opponent picks a card from the red pile, pronounces the word, and the first player tries to spell it correctly. If he succeeds, he advances his token one space. If he spells it incorrectly, he must move back one space. If the spinner lands on blue, the player can choose a card from either the blue or the red pile. Blue indicates moves of two spaces. Green means that the player can choose from any of the three piles; it indicates moves of three spaces. Thus a conservative player can always choose from the red pile which gives easy words but allows moves of only one space. He can move more rapidly by picking blue and green cards, but the words are more difficult, and the penalties are greater.

The pile of brown shortcut cards can only be chosen when a player lands on a shortcut square. If he spells the word on the brown card correctly, he may take the shortcut. If he misses, he must go back to the beginning and start again. When a player lands in the shortcut square, he has the option of picking a card from any one of the piles. If he picks from another pile, however, he may not take the shortcut. The game board is so arranged that any player may take only one shortcut at most during the game, and then only if he happens to land on the proper square. The word cards are changed periodically to give students practice with a large number of words. After the children have played the game a number of times, you can move words from a difficult pile to one which is considered less difficult.

This game may be modified to suit individual student needs. The only limitations are your imagination and the characteristics of the children. It should be modified from time to time in order to take advantage of the novelty effect.

Handwriting Skills Centers

Handwriting is another skills area which can be incorporated into a writing center. A quick check of the children's writing will undoubtedly turn up several letters that can be improved. Assignments should be individualized so that each child works only on those letters which he has trouble writing. A chart such as the one in Fig. 7-3 is helpful in keeping track of letters the children need to practice. As the teacher reads the children's assignments, she checks off on the chart the letters each child needs to practice. Use two colors of ink, one for lower case, and one for capitals. After the child has

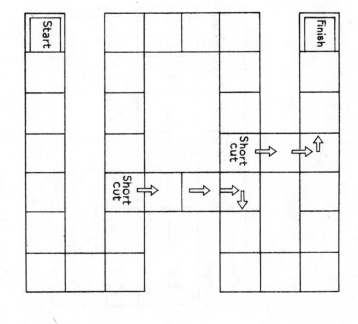

Fig. 7-2 *Road rally spelling*

practiced the particular letters he needs to work on, watch for improvement in his subsequent writing. When he improves sufficiently, cross off the check.

In conjunction with this handwriting practice, the children can use a visograph. Insert sample letters under the plastic cover and let the child trace over the letter a number of times using a grease pencil. Later, he can try writing the letter on clear acetate without using a model. With the visograph, the child can also trace sentences or short paragraphs in which the particular letters to be practiced appear frequently.

For practice, the child can write the sentences or the paragraph on paper in his best handwriting, or he may transcribe stories that have been dictated on tape, or rewrite stories that are presented in rough form.

Punctuation and Usage Skills Centers

Drill centers, whether for handwriting or punctuation, must be used with restraint. The connection between drill and application must always be made clear to the students. In many instances, children have trouble transferring what they have learned about punctuation and usage to their own writing. Many times they perceive practice in punctuation and usage as meaningless drill which has no value as far as their own communication is concerned. In order for these learning centers to be effective, it is necessary to help children understand how punctuation and usage skills relate to their own writing.

Name Letter	Louise	Tony	Joan	Ken	Margie	George
A a					✓	
B b		✓				
C c	✓			✓✓		
D d					✗	

FIG. 7-3 *Handwriting skills chart*

The teacher can begin by reading the children's stories in order to locate problem areas. Correction of these problems then becomes the objective. The objectives must grow out of the children's needs, not from the lessons in a curriculum guide or a grammar book. Although check tests should be included in the materials at the center, the final measure of mastery is the children's growth in written communication skills over the weeks and months of the school year.

The following example illustrates how to develop an objective based on a particular punctuation problem, to design appropriate learning center activities, and to assess progress. Imagine that the students have just written a story using direct dialogue. In examining their papers, you look specifically at the mechanics of how they write dialogue. You discover that a number of the children write indirect rather than direct dialogue, and set it off with quotation marks. Instead of *George said, "I like licorice ice cream."* they write, *"George said he likes licorice ice cream."* From these errors you derive the objective: the children will be able to write direct dialogue using quotation marks properly.

The comic strip approach (Fig. 7-4) can be used to teach toward the achievement of this objective. After a child fills in the blank bubbles over the heads of the characters, he writes the conversation on another piece of paper, substituting quotation marks for the comic strip bubbles and indicating each speaker by name. This objective can also be taught by having the child examine stories that are full of conversation. The child

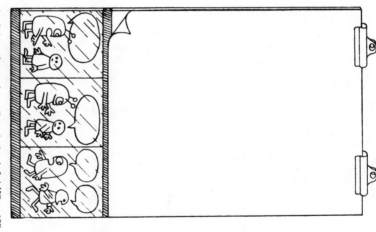

1. Cut a piece of cardboard about 8-1/2" x 15".
2. Cut a piece of acetate 4" x 8-1/2". Tape it to the cardboard along the top and bottom edges as shown. Insert a comic strip in the acetate pocket, covering the words in the bubbles.
3. The child attaches a 8-1/2" x 11" sheet of paper to the top of the cardboard with spring paper clips, then extends the balloons to his paper so he has room to write the conversation. He then removes his paper from the board.

FIG. 7-4 *Cartoon visograph*

reads several excerpts, then generalizes the characteristics of written conversation.

A magnetic board is a useful tool for analyzing written conversation. Write several sentences on stiff paper, then cut them into their individual elements. Make each word and each punctuation mark a separate item. Attach a piece of magnetic tape to the back of each card. Then place all the words on the magnetic board in random order. The child's task is to arrange the words and punctuation marks to make as many sentences, properly punctuated, as he can. It is helpful to have students work on this activity in small groups so they can help and check one another. Fig. 7-5 shows the words placed first at random, then in sentence form with the punctuation marks in place. The student could also have arranged the words to make this sentence: *"Let's eat, children," cried the Grandma.* After the student has tried out several combinations, he checks his sentence against a master list.

Creative Writing Centers

The methods of applying writing skills are endless. In addition to spelling and mechanics, the classroom should have centers devoted to creative writing in a variety of literary forms—narration, essay, description, haiku, riddles, and limericks. The listening and oral language centers that explore writing style can also be modified to serve as writing centers.

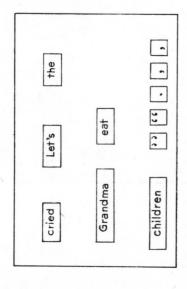
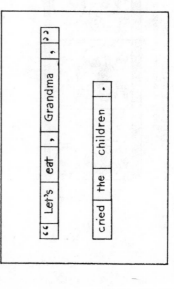

FIG. 7-5 *Punctuation practice*

The teacher's role in the creative writing center is to provide ideas and materials that motivate children to write. The more stimulating the center, the more frequently the child will want to write, and the more practice he will get.

The following materials can be used to motivate creative writing:

Task cards. The task cards used in oral language centers can be easily adapted for use in writing centers. Use story titles, beginning sentences, particular topics, a setting with a character and an event, or nonsense pictures with a task card attached.

Shape books. Put together twenty or thirty large sheets of paper (one for each child) and cut them in an appealing shape. The top sheet can be illustrated as appropriate. For example, one booklet might be cut in the shape of an elephant, as in Fig. 7-6.

A child opens the book to a blank page and writes a factual description of an elephant or an imaginative story, a poem, a limerick, a tall tale, or a legend about elephants. When the book is filled, the students read their contributions aloud to the class, then deposit the book in the classroom library. One variation of this idea uses geometric forms. The children write stories about the adventures of a circle or about things that are round. They might draw pictures of round objects and write stories about what they have drawn.

Abstract forms. Draw or paste a number of abstract forms on paper. The child uses the lines and angles as

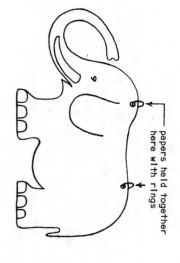

papers held together
here with rings

FIG. 7-6 *Shape book*

the basis of a drawing and writes a story about his picture.

What-if Stories. The children complete stories that start with a supposition: What if a unicorn came to live with you? What if all the clocks in the world stopped? What if the sky were red?

Collaborative stories. Two or three students pool their talents to write short stories. They choose their own topics and plots. (The learning that takes place through such collaboration often proves to be invaluable.)

Concluding Thoughts

The materials and activities for language arts instruction described in this chapter are by no means an exhaustive list. Using the basic activities presented here, however, you can expand your own program to incorporate a wide variety of objectives. Language arts skills pervade all areas of the curriculum. Spelling words and story topics alike can be designed to reflect all areas of student interest from art to zoology.

Selected References

Anderson, Paul S. *Language Skills in Elementary Education.* New York: The Macmillan Company, 1972.
This text covers language arts teaching in detail. It can serve as an excellent source of ideas and techniques, many of which can be incorporated into learning centers. It is a good source to consult when first setting up learning centers in the language arts because it helps the teacher determine her priorities.

Moffett, James. *A Student-centered Language Arts Curriculum, Grades K-6: A Handbook for Teachers.* Boston: Houghton Mifflin Company, 1968.
This book presents a rationale and a program for actively involving youngsters in language and language learning. In addition to presenting an overall program, it describes numerous activities designed to help children become competent in language arts, communication, and thinking skills. Activities, games, and devices are described, many of which lend themselves to a learning center approach.

Petty, Walter, and Mary Bowen. *Slithery Snakes and Other Aids to Children's Writings.* New York: Appleton-Century-Crofts, 1967.
Although not designed specifically for use in language arts learning centers, this book can serve as an excellent source of ideas for helping children become better writers. It presents ideas, topics, story beginnings, and objects which can be used to stimulate creative writing, descriptive writing, and writing forms. Proofreading activities which will fit into learning centers are also presented.

Platts, Mary E., and Sister Rose Marguerite. *Spice.* Stevensville, Mich.: Educational Services, Inc., 1960.

A wide variety of language arts activities for all elementary grade levels are included in this book. It is a useful reference for designing language arts learning centers.

Synectics, Inc. *Making It Strange*. Vols. 1-4. New York: Harper and Row, 1968.

Many ideas involving comparisons of incongruities and presentations of verbal patterns that stimulate imaginative speaking and writing are presented here. This is a source of numerous ideas for use in writing and oral language centers.

Walter, Nina Willis. *Let Them Write Poetry*. New York: Holt, Rinehart and Winston, 1962.

This book is a rich source of ideas for stimulating the writing of poetry. It describes how to set up an environment conducive to creativity, and suggests sources of inspiration and creative experiences. It discusses the subject matter of poetry, vocabulary building, and the evaluation of poetry. Many of the ideas can be incorporated into poetry centers.

8

Activities and Materials for Social Studies Instruction

THE ultimate goal of social studies instruction is an understanding of the individual and his role in society. In traditional classrooms where the child is asked to take his assigned seat, open his required text, and do the same assignment as everyone else, there is little opportunity to attain this broad goal. Classrooms that require the students to behave in a uniform and passive fashion (watching and listening, not doing and asking) are not representative of the varied world the children will face as adults. If we intend to teach children to appreciate the cultures and values of others, we must permit them to work together—to learn together—in the classroom.

Learning Contracts

Individualized instruction can be provided in the form of learning contracts. The contract in Fig. 8-1 was designed for a primary-class unit on Indians.

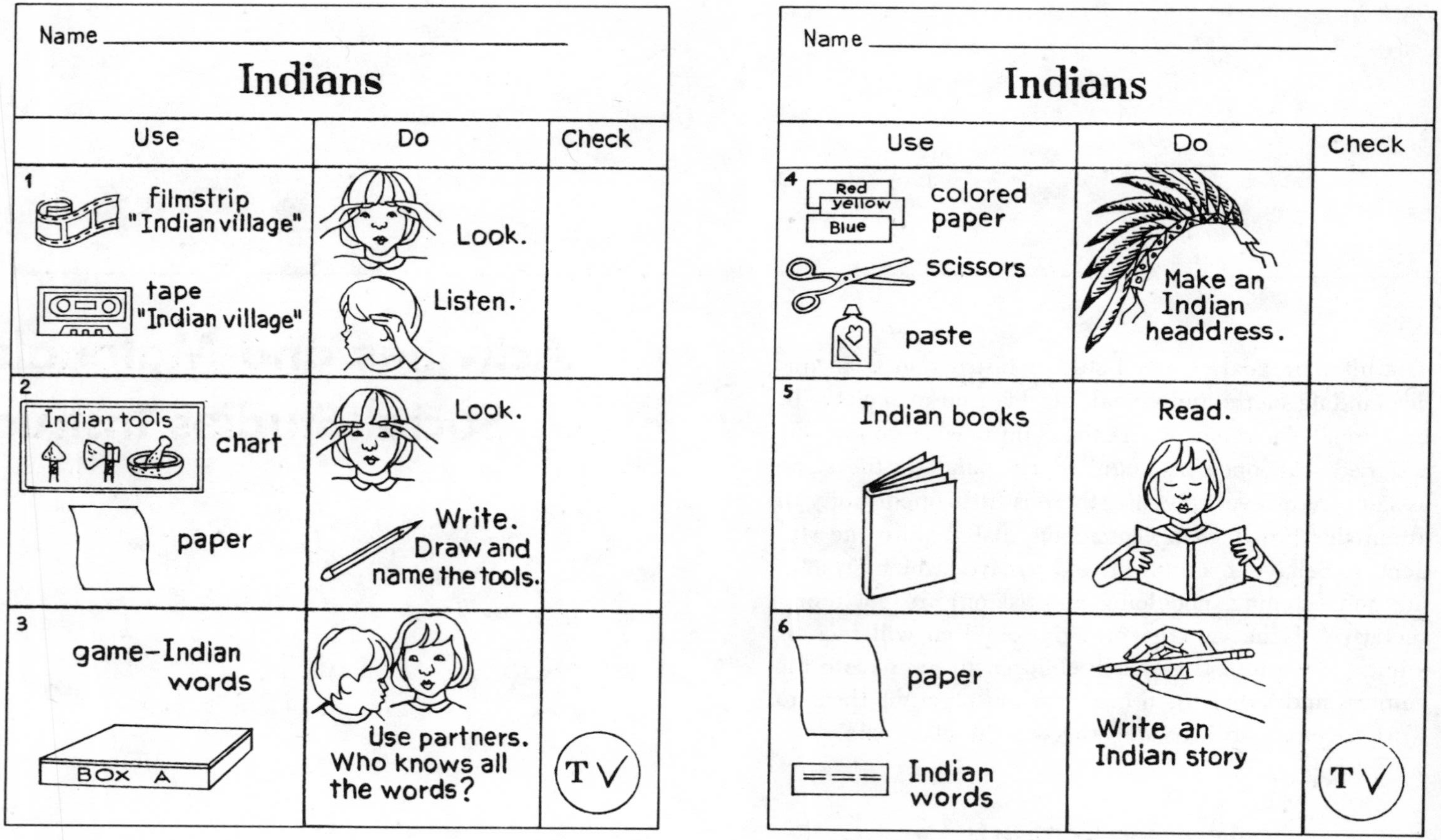

Name _____

Indians

	Use	Do	Check
1	filmstrip "Indian village" tape "Indian village"	Look. Listen.	
2	Indian tools chart paper	Look. Write. Draw and name the tools.	
3	game—Indian words Box A	Use partners. Who knows all the words?	TV

Name _____

Indians

	Use	Do	Check
4	colored paper (Red yellow Blue) scissors paste	Make an Indian headdress.	
5	Indian books	Read.	
6	paper Indian words	Write an Indian story	TV

Fig. 8-1 *Sample contract*

When a learning contract such as this is introduced in a primary classroom, it is essential to meet with the students to discuss the tasks. Go over the contract step by step, and encourage comments and questions. After this orientation session, the students are free to move around the room and investigate the materials that have been deposited at the various centers. Because only six learning centers have been set up for this particular unit, the children should distribute themselves so that all the materials are utilized and no center is overcrowded. Once they have decided where to work, the children discuss the tasks among themselves and decide how each one can best be accomplished. Together, they consider alternative approaches to each task, then establish their strategy.

Thus, even before they begin to work at the social studies centers, the children have practice in skills of decision-making and cooperation. As they form learning teams and approach the tasks as a group, the children learn how to work together toward a common goal, cooperating, yet allowing for individual differences. They learn to consider the teacher as a resource person and to call on her for assistance as necessary. If she, in turn, assumes the role of tutor and evaluator, it becomes easier for her to think of the children—their learning styles and their needs—in an individual manner. The classroom that provides this kind of environment is well on its way to attaining the broad goals of the social studies.

SOCIAL STUDIES INTEREST CENTERS

In any area of the social studies, an interest center can be used to introduce a unit and motivate study. This technique is particularly effective if you want the children to identify the goals. Pictures, maps, and realia of the country or culture under discussion can be displayed in a corner, along a wall, or on the bulletin board. Give the children ample time to browse through the interest center before they attempt the tasks.

As they explore the items on display, make note of questions the children raise. These will become the objectives for the unit. For example, a display showing realia from an African village might inspire the following questions: Why do they wear that kind of clothes? What do they grow to eat? Why are those musical sounds so different? What do the children do in school? Where do the fathers work?

Questions solicited from all members of the class can be written on slips of paper or on the chalkboard. The children then meet in a discussion group and organize the questions around common topics. The students may select the topics they wish to pursue. In this manner, students with mutual interests form a learning team. Work areas are selected next, and then the work begins.

First, the children must identify the ways and means of gathering information needed to answer their questions. Stock the centers with all the relevant realia, pictures, books, filmstrips, and other learning aids that can

The second unit, "The Story of Africa," uses a number of different techniques and media—reading, viewing, drawing, constructing, and listening.

A Task Card Unit: Exploring
Your Community and Other Communities

The objectives for this unit have been stated purposely in general terms to allow maximum opportunity for the child to develop attitudes about himself and how he relates to his environment and the society in which he lives.

OBJECTIVES: 1. To learn something about other communities as well as more about your own.

2. To discover that present conditions of growth and change have roots in the past.

3. To discover how cooperation enables people to meet their basic needs and results in better services for all.

4. To become aware of the role of informed citizens through the study of other communities or cities of the state, the nation, and the world.

5. To become aware of the origin and development of your own community.

possibly be provided. Suggest also that the children consult the library card catalog, the film order catalog, and other sources for additional information. In addition, it is often helpful to post a list of school resource persons that the children can call on for special assistance.

Working together, the members of each learning team draw up an outline of how they will approach the problem. The question of how to present the information must be answered next. Would a written report be best? Or would a poster, a diorama, or even a homemade film make a more effective presentation?

Encourage divergent thinking by listing alternate ways the students can develop reporting procedures. Throughout the unit, give high priority to independent decision-making and team interaction.

TEACHER-DIRECTED CENTERS

Not all teachers feel comfortable in the role of resource person. Often, a teacher may want to play a more active role in identifying the objectives and designing classroom activities. She may not be willing to let the children set the goals alone. This does not mean, however, that teacher-directed activities preclude a personalized, interactive learning environment.

The following two examples illustrate selected teacher-directed studies. The first one, "Exploring Your Community and Other Communities" (see Selected References), is designed for primary grades and uses task cards.

6. To discover how people in other communities are influenced by natural and cultural factors.

7. To learn how to use community maps to determine distance, direction, and location.

8. To learn how to use maps and globes to relate various areas of the world to current affairs.

9. To develop skills in using reference materials.

10. To practice making reports.

11. To form attitudes and strengthen values through learning the importance of cooperation and individual responsibility.

12. To develop increased understanding of, respect for, and loyalty to the American form of government.

PROCEDURE: Set up the learning center using task cards that are numbered and color-coded by centers. For each activity, materials are indicated by picture, symbol, or numerals. Many of the activities will be challenging, particularly to the advanced student. The activities are intended to enrich or extend the core ideas usually presented in social studies material at the primary level.

Red Center: Arts and Crafts Activities
1. Read Task Card #1.

Task Card #1   Red Center

Activity: Look at the study prints. *Geographical Regions of California* (15 prints). Start a picture file of some examples of different land forms in your community or state.

Materials: study prints, file box

---

2. Make diagrams showing how mountains differ from hills, coastal plains differ from desert plains, and valleys differ from plains.

3. Cut out magazine pictures of various types of housing that might be found in a suburb: tract homes, apartments, trailer parks, and so on.

4. Find pictures of people living on deserts in different parts of the world.

5. Find pictures of Indian and Mexican architecture.

6. List the services and commercial businesses that are essential to a suburb.

7. List and be able to discuss some of the old landmarks in your community—public buildings, private homes, parks, or locations where important events occurred.

8. Make a bulletin board display of newspaper articles about various types of public work projects underway in your community.

9. Use a flowchart to show how a product or raw material is transported from the dock to a city warehouse or processing center.

10. Paint a picture that expresses your ideas or feelings about the following types of transportation: monorails, ferry boats, subways, cable cars, trains. How does it feel to ride in an automobile in the heart of a large city, across a bridge, or through a long tunnel?

11. Be prepared to discuss ways that the appearance of your community could be improved. Sketch a plan to show the kinds of changes you would make.

Yellow Center: Music Activities

12. Listen to a selection of records that illustrate the music of cultures you have studied.

13. Choose one song, then use the appropriate rhythm instruments to accompany it.

14. Learn to play a song on a tonette or on melody bells.

15. Write an additional verse for a song you know.

Green Center: Science and Math Activities

16. Use an indoor sandbox and water to demonstrate how some land forms are made by rivers.

17. Discuss how climate may affect the animal and bird life found in a given area.

18. Use the mail order catalog to figure the cost of a year-round wardrobe for a boy or girl living in northern California.

19. Use the state road map to locate various Indian reservations.

Blue Center: Language Arts Activities

20. Write a story describing where you live. Include a description of the industries, business opportunities, and recreation facilities.

21. Find out about the kinds of jobs held by various groups of people within your community.

22. Contribute a recipe to a class cookbook of foreign foods. If possible, prepare the food at home and bring some to school to share.

23. Make plans for a vacation trip to a community you have studied. Compute the cost of food, shelter, entertainment, and car expenses.

24. Prepare a list of occupations which are (1) seasonal and (2) permanent in nature. Discuss the merits of each.

MATERIALS: Picture magazines, mail order catalogs, paper, pencils, crayons, paints, clay, papier mâché, table sandbox, study prints, library books, music books, films, filmstrips records, maps, picture atlas, social studies text, and teachers' guide.

RECORD KEEPING: Each child is responsible for keeping track of the activities he has completed. A checklist stapled to the inside of his pocket folder can hold his records and serve as a storage place for paper work. Folders can be filed in the back of the room when not in use.

A Media Center Unit: The Story of Africa

OBJECTIVES: 1. To demonstrate modes of living in various African communities.
2. To compare selected African cultures.
3. To grow in respect and appreciation of people from a different environment.
4. To present problems that have relevance to life in the world today.
5. To gain knowledge of transportation, communication, maps, and the history of Africa.

1: Stories of Africa

DESCRIPTION: A collection of twenty-nine stories on assorted topics are deposited at this center. Each story is accompanied by a colored-stamp picture and a large black-and-white picture.

MATERIALS: Two Golden Stamp Books, *Wonders of Africa*, mounted in acetate folders; ditto sheets with questions and activities for each story; pencils and other art supplies.

Outline for Unit in Africa

CENTER NUMBER	CENTER NAME	MATERIALS	DESCRIPTION
1	Crocodiles	African stories	Use to present facts about Africa's peoples, geography and animals.
2	Elephants	Maps	Use to teach map skills.
3	Sahara Club	Informative classroom picture series	Use for viewing and discussion of African life.
		Transparencies (4)	Use on an overhead projector to illustrate historical events.
4	Watusi Dancers	Records of Bantu music	Use to compose a musical score as a group. Construct bongo drums or other African musical instruments to accompany the record.
5	Lions	Sound filmstrip: *Africa, the Land of Developing Countries*	Use to accompany filmstrips and records.
		Ten filmstrips	Use for information, then follow up with a question-answer period. Students draw illustrations and do other appropriate art work.
		Outline maps of Africa	Use to show the important geographic features of each country.
6	Oasis	Supplementary materials	Use reading, games, puzzles, and boxes of African materials for supplementary activities.

ACTIVITIES: (Each day, the activity sheets will specify different art materials.)

2: Map Skills Study

DESCRIPTION: Twenty-seven pages of exercises explaining the use of globes and maps, determination of positions on maps and globes, as well as map scale and distances, keys and legends, and various symbols especially prepared for the fourth-grade level are deposited at this center. Answer keys are provided.

MATERIALS: Two copies of *Map Skills for Today* published by *My Weekly Reader*), paper, pencils.

ACTIVITIES: Study the information given, then answer the questions accompanying each assignment. Check your own answers.

3: Life in Africa

DESCRIPTION: Large pictures that accompany seventeen informative stories on African peoples, geography, wildlife, and occupations of the various industrialized and farming areas are deposited in this center, along with transparencies on geographical features, African races, and Africa's old and new nations.

MATERIALS: *Commercial Picture Series* or pictures of Africa, transparencies, overhead projector, outline maps of Africa, pens, ink, narrow-line marking pens, colored pencils.

ACTIVITIES: (Have a group leader read the information sheets accompanying the pictures, or have students take turns reading them. Show the pictures, then discuss the lesson.)

Locate and draw the Nile River valley. Color it blue. Locate the pyramids and draw them in as small brown triangles.

By coloring two maps, show the African races of 1000 A.D. and 1885.

Read the story of Dr. Livingston. Show on the map the journeys of both Stanley and Livingston. Make each route a different color.

Label the new African nations as of 1966 on your map (thirty-six countries).

4: Bantu Music

DESCRIPTION: This record of Bantu music was made in British East Africa. It captures the rhythms and tonal qualities of the music from this culture, and it teaches an awareness of different instruments and different methods of composition.

MATERIALS: Recording of folk and primitive music, information on the history of the instruments and songs, record player.

For each drum you'll need: one empty coffee can or cocoanut shell, sections of mailing tubes or short pieces of hollowed-out tree limbs not less than 4 inches in diameter, scraps of leather or chamois, string or leather shoe laces, two pieces of dowels or sticks of wood 6 inches long, and horns of cows or other animals. To assemble the drum, cover each end of the hollow tree limb with leather. Tie the leather in place by lacing it around the sides.

For writing rhythms, you'll need: paper with staff lines drawn in, red masking tape for notes, and acetate sheets to cover the staff lines.

ACTIVITY: Listen carefully to the record and identify the rhythmic patterns and tonal sounds. Try to compose a Bantu rhythm by tapping out a beat with your finger. Hum a tune to your rhythm. Remember not to go higher in scale than five notes. Record your tune on acetate sheets using tiny squares of red masking tape for notes. Make drums or other instruments. Play your song using drums or other instruments you have made.

5: Part I—The Developing African Nations

DESCRIPTION: This set of three records is correlated with six filmstrips. The record presents a narration while the students view the filmstrips. (You could use any set of commercial filmstrips for this center. Check local sources.)

MATERIALS: *Africa, the Land of Developing Countries,*[1] filmstrip projector.

[1]Slide Tours of the World, Panorama Division, Capitol Records, New York, NY.

ACTIVITY: View the films and listen to the recording. Answer the questions on the ditto sheets and check your answers with the key.

5: Part II—Ten Filmstrips on Africa

DESCRIPTION: *Transportation in Equatorial Africa,* Occupations in Equatorial Africa,* Native Tribes,* Modern Cities in Equatorial Africa,† An African Home Near the Equator,* Animals and Birds,† African Village Near the Equator,* Children of Equatorial Africa,* Farming in Africa,* Plants and Flowers.†*

MATERIALS: Construction paper, modeling clay or pottery clay, paints or crayons, pencils, filmstrip projector.

ACTIVITY: Show these filmstrips, then choose a chairman to lead a group discussion. Each student should submit two or three questions in writing and may call on others to give the answers. After viewing *Animals and Birds* and *Plants and Flowers,* some students may want to model animals in clay or paint birds and flowers.)

5: Part III—Maps of African Countries

DESCRIPTION: Outline maps of each country on ditto sheets.

MATERIALS: Dittoed maps, pens, colored pencils.

*Curriculum Films, Caswell C. Ellsins Co., Redondo Beach, CA.
†Encyclopedia Britannica Films, San Leandro, CA.

ACTIVITY: Using the World Book maps of African countries, select information on products, races of people, rivers, largest cities, animals, or other items of interest to add to the maps of each country. Sketch in the information first, then color it. What things of interest can you find? (This activity will give the children a chance to assume the initiative and responsibility for their own learning and to show whether they are able to gather information with a minimum of guidance.)

6: Bonus Center

DESCRIPTION: A collection of stories from books and pamphlets, illustrated magazine articles for fast learners to read and report on, and games such as bingo or cards, are available at this center. Some overhead transparencies showing artifacts can also be included. This material could also be used to teach early African history to the entire class at Center 5, Part III.

MATERIALS: Pictures, books, magazines, pamphlets, and games.

ACTIVITIES: (The activities will vary depending on which ones the pupil chooses.)

CLASSROOM ORGANIZATION

By way of introduction to this unit, the teacher can arrange a variety of African materials around the room. Displays on tables, shelves, and bulletin boards can all be used to illustrate facets of African life. After a day or two, when student interest is aroused, the class meets as a group to be briefed on the new topic. Classroom organization and behavioral standards should be discussed at this time. Following the planning period, the class views an introductory filmstrip on Africa.

To ensure leadership during the first stages of the unit, appoint the first committee chairmen yourself. The chairman will direct the activities of his group and operate audiovisual equipment when necessary. Later, the groups may choose new chairman themselves each week. It is often wise to appoint a substitute in case the chairman is absent or needs assistance.

Learning centers are identified by name—Sahara Club, Crocodiles, Elephants, Lions, Watusi Dancers, and Oasis Club. Cards printed with the names of the centers are posted daily in the pockets of an assignment chart. The materials should be extensive enough to cover five to six weeks of study.

The groups rotate centers daily, with one exception. There are five learning centers and one extra or bonus center. The bonus center contains a variety of activities to be used by those who finish the day's assignment early and are waiting for the rest of the group to catch up. In this way, all students can be occupied at all times. Students may select materials from the bonus center and return to work with their assigned groups. Advanced reading materials that challenge the fast learner can be kept here, along with simpler games for the slow learner.

In a class of thirty, six pupils can be assigned to each center. A checklist of the students' names and assignments is posted at each center, and as they complete assignments the students mark them with an "X". Assignments that remain unfinished are marked "/" at the end of the day, indicating that the task was begun. The chairman will then distribute that assignment again to the student on the following day.

As one means of maintaining interest, the teacher or a student with good reading ability can read to the entire class for five or ten minutes each day before the learning center activities begin. This period helps to settle the class and can serve as an excellent opportunity to bring out special points of interest, or have a discussion. This period can be especially helpful for those students who have reading difficulties.

The unit should end when most of the pupils have completed most of the activities, or when interest begins to lag. By the end of this unit, the students should have made a variety of African musical instruments and recorded a variety of African rhythms. The opportunity to share them with other classes will give the students a feeling of accomplishment. As a final project, the class might decide to stage a puppet show to summarize the unit and capitalize on their abilities to think and write creatively.

Concluding Thoughts

The richness and variety inherent in the social studies provides the most natural environment for the learning center style of teaching. Once it is organized, the individ-

ualized classroom promotes interaction among pupils. Nevertheless, the initial impetus towards learning centers must come from the teacher. The teacher who desires a learning center environment will find that she cannot rely entirely on the textbooks, teachers' manuals, and curriculum guides to provide the structure for her classroom. If she does, she may be faced with a restrictive classroom environment. Guides and manuals must be regarded as sources of material that can stimulate learning, not as ultimate answers. If a classroom is to function at its optimum level, then traditional time schedules, strict rules of behavior, and everyone-in-his-place thinking are no longer valid. Flexibility must prevail—and the teacher must plan for it. Flexibility does not mean random selection of learning tasks. Rather, the decisions for teaching and for learning should be made by teachers and students in order to achieve mutually defined objectives from a variety of rich materials and learning situations.

Selected References

Thady, Katherine. "Exploring Your Community and Other Communities." Unpublished manuscript. This unit was developed at San Jose State University under the direction of the author as a means of restructuring a primary classroom using learning centers and task cards.

Landess, Doris. "Story of Africa, Grade 4." Unpublished manuscript.

This unit was developed at San Jose State University under the direction of the author as a means of restructuring a fourth-grade classroom using learning centers and multi-media stations.

9

Practical Hints for Getting Started

THE classroom teacher who decides to implement learning centers must begin by redefining her role. Instead of setting herself up as the chief information officer, the teacher becomes the classroom manager. Prescription and individualized instruction assume top priority, and group lessons and information dissemination are played down. Record keeping, classroom organization, tutoring, and conferences occupy an increasingly greater portion of the teacher's time.

The student, on the other hand, becomes more actively involved in his own education. Instead of listening, reading, and writing on direction from the teacher, the child begins to make decisions on his own concerning what he will study, how he will report on it, when it will be due, and whom he will work with. He corrects much of his own work and files it in a folder. He learns to operate sound equipment, filmstrip viewers, and teaching machines as learning tools that complement the textbook. The student learns to work as a team member, instructing others, learning from others, cooperating with them, and respecting their individuality.

The classroom that uses learning centers will not be a quiet place. When children are actively involved and working together, the teacher should expect noise, movement, and discussion. Each teacher, each classroom, and each subject has its own level of noise tolerance. The noise level appropriate to any particular situation should be determined jointly by the teacher and the pupils. The noise in a working classroom should be controlled so that the children in one center are not disturbed by those in another. The teacher may decide to establish a quiet corner where children can go to work on tasks requiring more concentration.

The child who works at learning centers is no longer under the direct control of the teacher. He becomes more self-directed. He assumes a large share of the responsibility for his learning activities and his classroom behavior. In group situations, he learns to carry his share of the load. The learning centers, he finds, work for him only as much as he works for them. In this sense, his classroom with learning centers reflects the workaday world of his parents. Here, the student learns about the delicate balance between responsibilities and privileges. He will put this knowledge to use later as an informed citizen in a democracy.

Where to Begin

The first step in organizing classroom learning centers is to reorganize the materials. Begin by repackaging the usual units of instruction into a number of activity packets and depositing them at the centers. Next, reorganize the class into teams and send them to work at the centers. This laboratory approach allows the children to take more responsibility for independent decision-making. At the same time, it frees the teacher from large-group instruction and allows her to assume the role of learning catalyst. The move is complete when the children begin to use the centers as an assigned part of their studies. Any one of the following ideas can be used to introduce the new approach.

How to Begin

Drama Center

Place a large cardboard box—a Make-Believe Box—in a corner of the room behind a divider. Fill it with old clothes, hats, shoes, and uniforms. As the children finish their work, or on a rotating basis, they are free to dress up any way they wish and pantomime or role play for the others. This is a great way to instill self-confidence in the children while allowing them to use their excess energy constructively and creatively.

Buzy Box Center

Deposit all sorts of 3″ × 5″ task cards in this box. Illustrate the cards with flow pens and arrange them according to subject matter and difficulty. (*Example:* Turn to page 312 of the dictionary. Find a picture of different kinds of dogs. How are the dogs alike? How are they different? Find a way to show what you have learned to the class.) The objective here is to let the child choose and follow through with an activity that interests him. This procedure encourages self-direction.

Library Reading Center

Set up a small class library, classifying books by interest areas. Include old textbooks, paperback books, children's magazines, and books the children bring from home. Make a jacket for each book and write a short summary of the plot and a preview of the characters on the inside flap. Make a large poster explaining various ways of reporting or sharing books. (*Example:* Read your favorite part to the class, construct a diorama telling about your book, act out a scene from your book, design a jacket for your book, or tape-record your favorite part of the book.) Activities should cover everything from acting to writing.

Ecology Center

This area can be designed as an interest center, with a variety of books, filmstrips, tapes, charts, pictures, and objects for the students to examine. Encourage them to provide other materials for the center themselves, or to undertake a school or community project. Use large posters to illustrate current events related to pollution, recycling, and conservation.

Scrap Paper Art Center

This center can be a scavenger's paradise. Collect newsprint, multi-color ditto paper, construction paper, cellophane, tissue, old wallpaper, gift-wrapping paper, kitchen foil, and paper of every other imaginable weight and color. Place glue, glitter, paint, and scissors nearby. Give the children the freedom to make anything they please.

Pantomime Center

Make a set of 8″ × 10″ cards with pictures or drawings of animals or people pasted on each. They might represent characters from familiar stories or from real life. Children select several cards they like, then act out scenes using the characters they chose. You may want to include a few appropriate props so the children can represent their characters more realistically. Some children prefer to perform their parts wearing masks or using puppets. Pantomimes allow them to express their feeling through role playing with other children.

Math Center

All kinds of math skills can be practiced at this center. Deposit a balance scale, play money, blocks, dice, and games with markers and spaces on a table. Include old workbook pages and samples of ditto worksheets, too. At the primary level, the center can emphasize the skills of addition and subtraction. The simple act of rolling dice, for example, makes the practice of addition more fun. Or at the intermediate level the math center might be designed around the study of fractions. Supply the students with measuring devices such as rulers, cup measures, and spoon measures. You might develop a set of task cards to direct the children's explorations. (*Example*: Do you know how many ¼ cups equal 2 cups? Try to find the answer by filling 2 cups with ¼ cups at the sink.)

Listening Center

A record player or a tape recorder, a junction box, and several sets of earphones can be used at this center. If you only have a record player, place a selection of children's records in the center for the students to use. If a tape recorder is available, you can prepare read-along tapes of short children's stories for the students to listen to as they follow along in their books. Older children often like to prepare read-along tapes for listening centers in primary classrooms. Sometimes the children enjoy recording simple dialogue or stories they have written. Students with a journalistic bent may enjoy taking the tape recorder home to interview friends and family.

Music Center

Deposit all sorts of simple musical instruments here for the children to investigate. Let them use drums, flutes, and small pianos, as well as homemade instruments such as sandpaper blocks, sticks, rattles, and tambourines. Provide all the materials needed to construct the more simple percussion instruments. You may need students with measuring devices such as rulers, cup to suggest a few activities at first. Then allow the children to follow their own interests and invent their own instruments.

Sports Center

This learning center is made-to-order for the children who love sports but seldom have the opportunity to express their interest in the classroom. Stock it with books about sports stars, sports equipment, sports magazines, sports pages from the newspaper, and rule sheets for various games. Post charts showing the standings of favorite teams and players and let the students plot current standings as new data are gathered. The children may choose to write newscasts about sports events, do research on the history of a sport, write a biography of a great man of sports, or sketch a scale model of an olympic sports stadium.

Theme Center: Birds

Realia, pictures, filmstrips, and books about the theme —birds, in this case—are needed at this center. A wall chart can list suggestions of activities to help the children get started:

Look through the books. Draw a picture of an egg hatching.

Read books to find out where birds build their nests.

Read books to find out the different shapes of bird nests.

Read books to find out what materials birds use to build nests.

Build a bird house using construction paper. Follow the pattern.

Make a bird feeder from a milk carton.

Use the binoculars. Become a bird watcher.

Draw a bird.

Write a story, "If I Were A Bird."

Make a book of bird shapes.

Write a poem about a bird.

Choose a bird and find out where it lives and what it eats.

View a filmstrip and list five things you learned about birds.

Write a speech about your favorite bird.

Investigation Center

This center is designed to allow the children to "mess around" and find out how things work. Old electric irons, toasters, clocks, and parts from cars make ideal materials. The children will also need tools for investigating them—screwdrivers, pliers, end wrenches, hammers, and a magnifying glass. The activities at this center are undirected. Let the children tinker with the equipment as they want, play with the parts, and guess how they work.

Language Master Center

A language master machine can become a center in itself. Use cards with magnetic strips attached for recording short phrases for individual listening. The vocabulary lists for a social studies unit, for example, can be presented on the cards along with illustrations and definitions. Students use the machine individually. They see the word, hear the word, say the word, then play back their recording. Individual spelling lists, math facts, phonics work, and similar materials can also be developed using this machine.

Centers for the Physical Education Program

By dividing the class into a number of small groups you can introduce several physical education games or skills at once. Exercises such as those from the President's physical fitness program are a good place to begin. Once it has learned its exercise, each group in turn teaches it to the others. The students not only only act as instructors, but also record the progress of their peers.

Drama Center

Flannelboards, felt cutouts, magazines for cutting, a puppet theater, materials for making puppets, makeup, Halloween masks, and a colorful array of hats are some of the props that children enjoy working with in the drama center. This is more than a place for free play, however. The children write and direct their own productions here. Students in the upper grades are especially capable of this type of activity. The drama center provides a constructive outlet for the children's robust energy.

Skill and Game Center

Students can help to stock this center by bringing all kinds of commercial games to school on loan from their homes. You can contribute puzzles, teacher-made games, pages from workbooks, and other items from the supply room. Once the games have been gathered, take inventory to identify the kinds of skills each one entails. Using this information, assign the games on a prescription basis to children with those particular needs. The center can also be used just for enjoyment. A child can come here on his own to play a game with a friend or with the teacher.

Poetry Center

Books of poetry, rhyming games, word lists, picture films, poetry starters, poems written by other children, and poems to be copied into individual booklets are the basis of this center. Let your imagination guide you in selecting materials. You might want to choose a poet of the week, for example, and send his work to the local newspaper or publish it in the school bulletin.

Personal Book Conference

Each child selects a book that interests him from the ones at school or at home. Next, he arranges a conference with you. Together, you look through the book, its pictures and its headings. To help the child get started, you might point out the key characters, note new vocabulary words, and ask motivating questions. Then set a date for a second conference. By that date, the child must have read all or part of the book and be ready to share it with you. In turn, you might share with the child a book that you are reading. The purpose of the conference extends beyond a check of the child's comprehension to a mutual display of interest in books and the world of reading.

Programmed Materials Center

Several commercial programmed textbooks in reading and mathematics are now available for classroom use. A programmed text provides immediate feedback to the child by requiring him to make many choices and to check his own work. Often, problems are worked on the left side of the page, and the answers are listed on the right. Many children become fascinated by this format and will work steadily for long periods of time. They progress at their own speed. Simply deposit programmed materials here in their entirety, or cut them into small units and staple them into colored folders. In this manner, many short units can be made from a few complete texts, allowing several children to work at the center simultaneously.

Sounds Center

Children in the primary grades can be introduced to phonics at a sounds center. Deposit several mirrors here, along with phonics worksheets, anagrams, displays of letter blends, ditto practice pages, and answer keys. As the children practice making the sounds, they can watch their faces in the mirrors.

Science Table

A box of simple, inexpensive science equipment is all that is required at this center. Basic items include batteries, wire, magnets, scales, books, pieces of metal, washers, bottles, cans and litmus paper. To direct the child's investigations, make a numbered card file of suggested experiments and ideas for collections and exhibits. When the child completes an investigation, he prepares a short report using the file number of the card to identify his work. His report may take the form of a written analysis, an oral presentation, a graph, a wall chart, or a model.

Construction Table

This center is completely open-ended. The child chooses from a stack of materials and constructs whatever he wants. Scraps of wood, wallpaper, tile, scissors, glue, saws, hammers, and nails are all basic construction equipment. Given a free hand, most children find this center engrossing.

Private Writing File

Set up a box or file drawer at this center and assign each child his own personal writing folder or envelope. Whenever he wants, the child can write personal messages or short stories to you, assured that only you will ever see or read them. The file becomes a strictly private communication between child and teacher. If a child's writing requires a reply, you can write an answer in his folder. The child can use his private file daily, or not at all.

Art Center

The art center presents a viable alternative to large-group art projects. By alternating projects at the center, it is possible to introduce a variety of techniques and to give the children a choice of activities. For a start, choose four or five different art projects, such as torn tissue paper collage, crayon resist sketches, straw-blown ink pictures, and stick-and-ink drawings. Post a sample of each technique in the center, along with the directions and materials. Let the children come to the center a few at a time and choose the projects they want to try. If the number of students working here is kept to a minimum, the need for elaborate preparation and cleanup is nearly eliminated.

A Quiet Corner

Set up a table and some comfortable chairs in this corner. A bookcase along one wall or a drape suspended from the ceiling makes this place a secluded nook. You might deposit a few quiet games here, such as jigsaw puzzles, crossword puzzles, books, crayons, paper, clay, or playing cards. A child comes to the center to be by himself. No one talks in the quiet corner. It is a place to think, to daydream, or just to look out the window for a few minutes of quiet reflection.

Choose Your Own Topic Center

Arrange an assortment of objects—peanut, screw, clothespin, toothpick, penny, foreign coin, feather—pictures, and a list of topics on a table. The children may choose one object or picture and write a story about it, fiction, nonfiction, biographical, or science fiction.

Map Center

Display various types of maps at this center, relief, area, physical, outline, rainfall, political, and special products. Commercial maps and maps clipped from magazines and newspapers can also be used. Encourage the children to examine the ones that interest them and choose an assignment from among the task cards that are filed nearby in a large envelope. The tasks should range from simple to complex. The card might suggest that the child copy a map and write a description of it, or that he make a salt-and-flour map, draw a map of his school, neighborhood, or city, invent a game using maps, use an opaque projector to enlarge a portion of a map, or compare and contrast selected maps.

History Play Center

You'll need a number of books on a historical topic—biographies, diaries, documents, and texts—along with period props such as clothes, hats, and weapons. The children choose the characters they want to portray and write the dialogue for them. After a few rehearsals, they may want to present their interpretation to the class. This center is particularly effective as part of a social studies unit.

Religion Center

Religions of the world can be introduced to students through books, articles, and pictures. Gather copies of the Bible, The Koran, and other basic religious texts for this center. Filmstrips also make excellent resources. *National Geographic Magazine*, *Life*, and other periodicals often print large, colorful pictures and articles on the religions of other cultures. Using these materials, the children might develop strip-story murals comparing significant events in selected religions. They might also compare the music of different religions by singing or chanting representative rituals and recording them on tape. A field trip to a passion play or a religious pilgrimage might be included in this course of study.

Inquiry Table

Several sheets of paper, each with four or five related questions on topics from current events, history, literature, or science are the basis of this center. File them in a manila folder. List references and resource materials beside each set of questions. Direct the students to find the answers through individual research. If the questions pertain to science experiments, or if the projects require interviewing or taking surveys, students can project when they will have the results and plan to deposit them in the center at a certain date.

Buddy System

Within a classroom based on the learning center approach, a buddy system can provide a basic organization for ready assistance and team learning. Determine the

basis for teaming after considering the child's academic strengths and weaknesses, social leadership, and creative energies. In addition to helping each other periodically when the need arises, the buddies can work together on specific activities. You can develop a list of special activities just for buddies and let them work together once or twice a week.

Discovery Day

On a given day every three weeks or so, organize a discovery-centered activity. One investigation might include a walk through the school visiting other classrooms, the office, the principal, the custodian, the nurse, and other personnel. The children look for "discoveries," interesting facts or bits of information they come across. Other discovery days can be spent in the library, walking through the neighborhood, or visiting a nearby office or business. Together, parents, students, and teachers can supply the classroom with all kinds of items around a chosen theme: vacations or visits, games and toys from home, tools we use at home and school, foods of other lands, or the cars we drive.

Primary Source Research Center

A prominent poster in one corner of the room declares the theme of this center. It might be crime, racial understanding, world travel, presidential elections, or foreign countries. The children search primary sources such as the newspaper, magazines, speeches, television, radio, or documents for pertinent information. In the center they post the items they find, either transcribed or in the original form. Each child must write a caption of a few key words beside the items he contributes. After a week or so of research, combine the key topics into a group booklet with the primary sources included as exhibits or illustrations.

Open-ended Stories Center

Stories of all sorts are suitable for this activity—all you have to do is remove the ending. This can be done in several ways. You can clip off the ending of a magazine story, cover the ending of a textbook story with a piece of paper, photocopy a story leaving out the last page, or tape record a story omitting the ending. At the learning center the children complete the story by writing an ending for it, acting it out, or recording it on tape. After several alternative endings have been developed, deposit them all in an envelope at the center so the children can read what the others have written. This activity is most effective when children have studied writing techniques and can identify the elements that comprise an effective ending. Key words that identify these elements can be posted in the center for reference as the children work. After a little practice, children can learn to select their own stories for the center, having decided what parts to omit.

Chalkboard Center

Students can use the chalkboard during seatwork time or on a rotating schedule set up for independent writing activity. They can copy words, practice letter formation, write an original story, or copy a poem for the class. Word puzzles, cross-number puzzles, and math number sequences can also be supplied at this center. You might attach a colorful picture or painting to the chalkboard for the children to examine and use in connection with a writing activity, such as naming descriptive words. Colored chalk can be a powerful motivational tool. Color can be used to emphasize differences or similarities in rhyme schemes, root words, or syllables. One section of the chalkboard can be reserved each day for an individual child to write a story. Frame this section with strips of colored paper or stripes of colored chalk and label it *Author*, followed by the child's name.

Modified Writing Center

A supply of blank books with attractive covers can motivate almost every child to write stories. Give them inviting titles that each child can interpret in his own way, such as "Tall Tales," "What I Have Discovered," or "The Worst Thing That Ever Happened to Me." Decorate the covers with magazine pictures, or cut them in irregular shapes (triangles or diamonds) or in the shapes of objects (flowers, cars, houses, or animals). A piece of paper folded in thirds makes another effective kind of booklet. Paste a picture to represent the beginning of a story, and another picture on the third section to tell what happens at the end. The child writes the middle of the story on the center section.[1] Keep simple and more advanced dictionaries at this center.

Shapes Center

This center is developed for the purpose of teaching geometric shapes through independent study. Make a number of envelope packets, one for each selected shape. The triangles envelope, for example, contains pictures of different triangles and cutouts of small and large triangles, scalene, obtuse, right, isoceles, and equilateral. Deposit several geoboards in the center. (These are 12″ × 12″ boards with 10 × 10 rows of wire brads spaced one inch apart.) The child uses rubber bands or stretchable colored yarns to replicate geometric shapes on the board. As another activity, the child can search through old magazines looking for the shape he is studying. When he finds an example, he cuts it out and pastes it on a large piece of paper. By the time he has worked through each envelope he will have his own shapes booklet with a page for each shape he knows.

[1]For other ideas, consult R. Van Allen, *Language Experiences in Early Childhood* (Chicago: Encyclopedia Britannica Press, 1969).

Transparency Center

Children can prepare their own transparencies for overhead projection to show the class something interesting they have learned. Provide them with sheets of plastic acetate, colored flow pens, and templates for letters and shapes. Give them plenty of time to experiment and create. They can wash off ink from flow pens with water if they want to begin again. The challenge of drawing transparencies gives students an opportunity to record personal interpretations.

Read-to-a-Partner Center

At this center, the children select a partner and a story they want to read, then they take turns reading to each other. They may like to lie on the floor or retire to a comfortable corner for this activity. You can write a list of questions on the chalkboard to guide their reading. In some cases, you might assign one child to act as the teacher for another. Or you might join the activity yourself by choosing a book to share and read with several children.

Quest Center

When a child finds a topic in his regular assignments that is of deep and genuine concern to him, give him the opportunity to study it in depth by moving him from his regular position into the quest corner. Excuse him from the regular assignments so he is free to follow his interests. For example, if a child becomes especially interested in electricity, he can spend time studying it in depth using a variety of media. In addition to books and magazines, the child should be given access to film and filmstrip catalogues so he can order some that pertain to his topic. Similarly, models from curriculum materials centers and laboratory experiment manuals should be made available to the child. Using all these resources, the child develops several projects or reports on his topic—he becomes the class expert on electricity. If two students have the same interests, they can help one another.

Individualized Programs

Individualized Spelling

Words for the individualized spelling program can be gathered from a variety of sources. Above all, the words should be of personal interest to the child who studies them. For each child, develop a list of words that ranges from easy to difficult and that includes all parts of speech. Use words from all subject areas and activities that are connected with a school day. Words can also come from the individual child, his interests, and his extra-curricular activities, his reading and his writing. Keep track of words the child uses and misspells—his personal problem words—and write each one on a card. The child then files the cards in a personal word box that he decorates himself.

Each child is responsible for learning a given number of these words each week, and he chooses his own list. Use a chart to suggest alternate ways of learning the words. They might use all the words in a story, make a vocabulary list with definitions, use them in sentences, or make crossword puzzles with them. Some children may like to choose spelling partners and dictate their lists to one another. Whichever method he chooses, the child must make a personal commitment to learn the words. When the child has learned a word, he moves it to a part of his personal word box marked Mastery Words. If he fails to master some words, he puts them on a list for the following week or discusses the problem with you in a conference.

Personalized Reading

Books on a wide range of topics at a wide range of reading levels are needed at the reading center. These include developmental reader textbooks, library books, paperback books, and children's personal books. Instead of following along page by page in an assigned textbook, the children read the books they choose. You will need to sequence the reading skills and pretest the children in order to determine their reading levels and the particular skills they need to practice. For general reading and comprehension, the child should choose a book that is in his reading range or easier. Sometimes the easier book is the best choice because it will improve both his fluency and his speed. Guided by the pretest information, develop an individual folder of appropriate skill work for each child. Write individual prescriptions for the children using activity sheets, ditto materials, pages from workbooks, and an assortment of other materials. File them in individual folders. Children with similar needs may be grouped together for instruction.

Confer with each child on an individual basis several times a week to share his progress and to give him additional assignments. The conference gives the child a chance to express his reading interests, and you have a chance to check his comprehension and vocabulary. In the conference, the child discusses the book he is reading. You might ask him to talk about one part in detail, to read aloud his favorite part, or to summarize the events of a certain section. Students keep track of the titles and authors of the books they read and the dates they start and finish them.

It is helpful to post a chart listing ways the children can share their books using dioramas, filmstrips, oral reports, posters, bulletin boards, character diaries, or prepared book report forms. When a child finishes reading a book, he chooses one of these methods to report on it.

Developmental Math

Through an investigation of several arithmetic textbooks, develop a checklist of specific arithmetic topics that need to be learned immediately above, below, and at grade level. Next, administer a pretest to the entire class. Textbook review sections and chapter tests are suitable for this purpose. From the test results, you can identify each child's strengths and weaknesses.

The next step is to duplicate the checklist and staple a copy into the front of a personal mathematics folder for each child. Check off the areas of mastery and write individual assignments for each child based on his needs.

Individual prescriptions list the pages to be worked, projects and activities to be completed, and the form that reports should follow. When appropriate, give the child access to answer books or keys so he can check his own work. You can check summary pages and tests yourself. In order to build a supply of material for individual prescriptions, you will need new, supplementary, and old textbooks. Classify these and other materials by skill—story problems using division, for example, or drill problems in whole-number addition.

As he works on his individual activities, the child can refer easily to the appropriate books and pages he needs to work on. When he feels he is ready, he takes a mastery test. These tests may be either commercially prepared or teacher-made. If he has mastered the particular skill, he moves on to the next area indicated on his checklist.

For children who need to use other media in addition to pencil-and-paper activities, you can provide filmstrips, practice records, transparencies, an abacus, feltboard figures, or other manipulative devices. Include them on the children's prescriptions.

For nondevelopmental topics such as measures, geometry, or number pattern exploration, you can create a variety of task cards. List one activity on each card, then file the cards in boxes and deposit them in the appropriate centers along with the required materials. The children choose the cards they like and work on them with partners. Plan to devote at least one day per week to nondevelopmental tasks.

Individualized Social Studies

Arrange regular class units on themes such as the farm or explorers of the West into centers for the following basic activities: writing, research, art, listening, maps, and filmstrips. Staple a checklist of all the activities in each center into the front of each child's folder. Introduce the centers to the children before they begin to work, then allow them to move from center to center, following their prescriptions and checking off the activities they complete. By allowing them a free choice of activities, it is possible to compensate for individual differences in learning rates and interests.

You can also give the children a choice of methods of reporting on their research activities. They can draw, write, design a transparency, make a tape recording, or construct a model. They will need to confer with you about the method they wish to use and the procedures they will follow. You may wish to use large groups for introducing a unit or reviewing it, and for role playing. Children progress through all other activities at their own pace.

Let the students file completed work in their folders. If possible, check and evaluate it in individual conferences with them. You can deposit in-depth study units and paper-and-pencil tests in a test box.

Weekly Contracts

Learning contracts are another way of individualizing either one subject or the entire curriculum. Give each child a number of tasks to be finished during the week. Write each task on a contract using pictures, numerals, and short phrases to identify the learning situations. The contract in Fig. 9-1 is designed to be used one period per week, or whenever the child is not working on regular assignments. At each of the centers, post a large butcher paper chart with the same phrase or illustrations used to refer to it in the contract. For example, an enlarged copy of frame 10, "Show how our fish breathes," is also tacked over the fishtank at the science center.

Monday morning is an ideal time to introduce the contracts. Discuss each frame with the children, then let them choose where they want to begin. If you want all the students to do certain frames, key them with a big star or other mark. Mark a large "T" (for teacher) on the frames you want to check yourself. Use other symbols as necessary. On Friday, there should be time for everyone to evaluate the week's work. If the children had difficulty with one frame, or if they showed unusual interest in another, you might want to include that frame on the next week's contract. Blank or open frames can be included, too, so the children have a chance to design their own learning tasks. The type of freedom that learning contracts provide encourages the children to become responsible, self-directed students.

Concluding Thoughts

The transition from traditional teaching methods to personalized instruction at classroom learning centers will be most successful if you consider the following points:

1. Give the children as much freedom as possible in the selection of materials and tasks.
2. Allow them freedom of movement and communication so they can gather the materials they need, organize them, and set to work in groups or alone, without supervision.
3. Set up a flexible schedule that allows the children to work on things they need to learn and want to learn.
4. Keep assignments open-ended to encourage in-depth study.

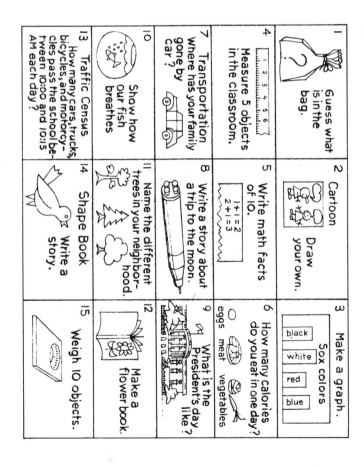

Fig. 9-1 *Weekly contract*

5. Let the children check their own work and test themselves so that they can get immediate feedback on their progress.

6. Develop a system of record keeping that the children can use on their own.

7. Develop a classroom environment rich in stimuli that interest the children and encourage them to pursue their own interests.

8. Confer with the children often on an individual basis in order to truly personalize instruction.